FOOTPRINTS ON AFRICAN HEARTS AND LANDS

THE LIFE AND WORK OF

Dr. Samuel W. Hynd

GWEN ELLIS WITH ELIZABETH HYND

TRIBUTES TO
DR. SAMUEL HYND

As a young medical student, I came to Swaziland to study tropical medicine and was mentored by Dr. Samuel Hynd. Little did I know how much my life would be impacted and inspired by this humble doctor with a huge heart. Following my training, I founded an international medical organization that has taken Dr. Hynd's compassion for the suffering to people throughout the world. Many years later, I returned to Swaziland and found Dr. Hynd where I had last seen him—seeing patients in the very clinic where he had mentored me. I know of no person who is more deserving of Jesus' words, "Well done, thou good and faithful servant."

Gary Morsch, MD
Founder, Heart to Heart International

Dr. Hynd is a God-fearing man who has shown great commitment in the work he does, ensuring that Swazis worship our Almighty God in healthy bodies and with sound minds. This ensures a holistic approach to human development. As one of the longest serving missionaries in Swaziland, he, through his healthy relations with the church and other government ministries, has been of great influence in the establishment of many mission schools, health centres, clinics, and churches around the country.

A very thoughtful, knowledgeable, and professional man, blessed with exceptional skills, especially in his technical area of expertise. He always shows love to the people, caring more for them and about them than he does about himself. He allows his co-workers time for lunch while dedicating his own lunchtime towards making a difference in the lives of others.

Dr. Samuel Hynd is a true son of the Kingdom of eSwatini (Swaziland). He has done every Swazi citizen a great service by sharing in an all-inclusive manner and courageously working in the country, thus earning awards from the relevant powers both in the country and beyond.

To make mention of a few honors of significance: In September 2001, the University of Swaziland conferred upon Dr. Samuel W. Hynd the Degree of "Doctor of Science *Honoris Causa*" for his exceptional professional service in the Kingdom of Swaziland.

In 2008, the Head of State and sovereign monarch of the Kingdom of Swaziland, His Majesty King Mswati III, authorized him to have, hold, and enjoy the dignity and rank of "Commander of the Order of Eswatini."

In 1998 the sovereign monarch and Head of State of the United Kingdom of Great Britain, Her Majesty Queen Elizabeth II, nominated and appointed him "Commander of the Civil Division of the Most Excellent Order of the British Empire."

As a pastor in the Church of the Nazarene, I have been privileged and humbled to know Dr. Hynd as both a man of God and a medical practitioner.

Reverend Grace Masilela
Pastor of the Mbabane Church of the Nazarene
Trustee to His Majesty King Mswati III

Dr. Samuel W. Hynd is a living legend. His remarkable life of service and ministry, which has touched the lives of many in Swaziland, Scotland, and around the world, follows the significant contributions made to Christ and the Church by his grandfather and father. This book traces this goodly heritage and is an account of decades of service to Christ, to the Church of the Nazarene, and to the Kingdom of Swaziland. Dr. Hynd's life demonstrates faithfulness to Christ through triumph and tragedy, and is an example of untiring commitment to the work of the church and of a keen interest in people. It will be a blessing, encouragement, and inspiration, to all who read it. Thank you, Dr. Hynd, for your life of service and dedication to Christ, for your faithfulness to the Church, and for your friendship and fellowship.

Reverend Colin H. Wood
Former District Superintendent—Church of the Nazarene
Former Pastor—Sharpe Memorial Church of the Nazarene, Glasgow, Scotland

The arrival of the Hynd Family in Swaziland was a blessing to the Kingdom of Swaziland. The Hynd Family helped to spread the Word of God to the Swazi Nation; they established the Raleigh Fitkin Memorial Hospital in the centre of the country and established schools and clinics all over the Nation. These facilities covered many parts of the Kingdom of Swaziland. The schools grew from one small primary school, which after some years developed into a fully-fledged High School, and now a University has been added. The Raleigh Fitkin Memorial Hospital provided medical services to a large section of the Swazi population that came from all the regions of Swaziland.

I spent my first years of schooling at Ezulwini Primary School. When I joined the Nazarene Primary School in 1942, I was eleven years old. At the time, Samuel Hynd was in boarding school at St. Marks Secondary School in Mbabane. He later studied medicine enabling him to join the family team at the RFM Hospital where he was to make a tremendous contribution to the Nation including the Royal family.

The Swazi people received much help through the Hynd family and other missionaries preaching of the Word of God and providing medical, religious, and educational facilities. The Hynd Family gained great importance and became the symbol of the development of these institutions, making the family famous until even the current national education curriculum includes their legacy.

His Majesty King Mswati III realized the role played by the Hynd Family and soon appointed Dr. Samuel Hynd as Minister of Health between 1978-1982. As Minister of Health, Dr. Hynd, who spoke siSwati fluently, opened many primary health care centers and clinics around the country. Dr. Hynd also founded a number of Non-Governmental Organizations, which contributed immensely to the development and improvement of lives and the livelihood of many Swazis—CANGO (Coordinating Assembly of Non-Governmental Organizations), COSAD (Council on Smoking Alcohol and Drugs), and ACAT (Africa Co-operative Agricultural Trust). I was involved with ACAT as a board member and was part of the national improvement of agricultural services in multiple communities throughout the country as they organized themselves in ACAT groups. It has been my lifetime privilege to serve together with my dear friend and colleague, Dr. Samuel Hynd.

Dr. Ben Mshamndane Nsibandze

Former Deputy Prime Minister
Retired Hhohho Regional Administrator
Former Director of the National World Food Programme
Former Director of the National Disaster Programme
Board Member of ACAT
Indvuna (Headman) of Elwandle Community in Manzini Region

My first visit to Swaziland was in 2006 when I spent my very first day in country with Dr. Samuel Hynd. I had heard much of this great man over the years but was blessed finally to meet him and witness firsthand a life lived for others and for the Nation of Swaziland. From serving as the Swazi Minister of Health to Chief Medical Officer at Raleigh Fitkin Memorial Hospital to founding the ACTS II AIDS Clinic in his 80's, his legacy continues to challenge and inspire all around him, including me.

Barbi Moore

Director of Global Outreach
Bethany First Church of the Nazarene
Bethany, Oklahoma

The Bible says in Romans 8:28, *And we know that all things work together for good to them that love God, to them who are the called according to his purpose.* I have seen this scripture working in *Babe* Grandpa (*Mkhulu*) Hynd's life. God called him to the people of Swaziland, and he came giving them hope, love, and health. God is still working through him. He lives and moves with God, Who has provided him with everything he needs. How good and pleasant it is to know Dr. Samuel Hynd. He is an example of someone who listens to God and who walks according to God's purposes. I want to walk with God the way he has. When I do, I know everything will work together for good for me and for anyone who reads this book. Walk with God and your life will be changed. I am so blessed to have the pleasure of calling Dr. Samuel W. Hynd, *"Babe."*

Caleb Abraham

Eldest son in the New Hope Centre family
University of Pretoria student studying for a social work degree

The story is told of a little girl whose father had just become a Doctor of Philosophy. "So," a friend said to her, "Your daddy is now a doctor." "Ah yes," said the little girl, "but he's not the kind of doctor who helps people!"

Dr. Samuel Hynd is the kind of doctor who helps people. His whole adult life has been spent in caring for the bodies and souls of men, women, and children. To see Dr. Hynd in his clinic was not only to receive treatment for the body but wise counsel—medicine for the soul.

Dr. Samuel Hynd was born in Scotland in the home of his maternal grandparents, Dr. and Mrs. George Sharpe, the founders of the Church of the Nazarene in the United Kingdom. His parents, David and Kanema Hynd graduated from Glasgow University. His father, David, returned to study medicine specifically to come to Swaziland to found the new Nazarene Mission Hospital in Manzini. Samuel Hynd arrived in Swaziland at the age of five months with his parents and older sister, Isabel. He grew up as a "white Swazi." His father spoke Zulu with a strong Scottish accent, but Doctor Samuel grew up speaking siSwati fluently. Apart from his return to Glasgow for his own medical studies, he has lived in Swaziland now for ninety years.

Dr. Samuel joined his father on the staff of the Raleigh Fitkin Memorial Hospital in 1950. (His younger sister in this remarkable family, Dr. Margaret Hynd, also became a medical missionary.) Eventually, after his father's retirement, he became the head of the mission station and was the entrepreneur who built the splendid new hospital, one of the most advanced mission hospitals in Africa when it was opened. At the same time, he suffered the tragic death of his dear wife, Rosemarie, and the pain of leaving the mission station to which he and his parents had devoted so many decades. He subsequently served as Minister of Health in the government of the newly independent Swaziland under King Sobhuza II. He was physician to the Royal family for many years, supervising the birth of the present king, His Majesty King Mswati III. His six decades of service to the Swazi people have been recognized by the conferring of the honorary degree of Doctor of Science by the University of Swaziland, and also, since Swaziland is a member of the Commonwealth, by the conferring of the Commander of the British Empire by the Head of the Commonwealth, Queen Elizabeth II, at a ceremony at Buckingham Palace in London.

As well as being an entrepreneur and administrator, his greatest service has surely been that, like his Master, he has not only been a preacher of the Gospel, but a physician and counselor to thousands. After leaving the Ministry of Health, he continued his own medical practice, ably supported by his new wife, Phyllis McNeil.

Even after retiring from his own medical practice in his eighties, he has spearheaded the creation of a new clinic to cope with the HIV/AIDs pandemic.

My own family has been associated with Dr. Hynd's family for over a century. Both my grandfathers were laymen under the ministry of Dr. Sharpe and my father, Arthur Noble, was Dr. Samuel's best man at his wedding to Rosemarie Ballard. So it is a particular pleasure to contribute an endorsement to this book. It is a heart-warming account of his life. Dr. Elizabeth Hynd has contributed much of the history and information used to create this book. While she is a Doctor of Philosophy and not of Medicine, she also helps people!

The story told in these pages will move readers to give thanks to God for the great example Dr. Hynd has set for Christians in every walk of life. But more than that, the book will challenge us to follow in Dr. Hynd's footsteps as he has followed in those of the Lord Jesus, by consecrating ourselves fully to the Lord who gave all for us.

Thomas A. Noble

Professor of Theology,
Nazarene Theological Seminary, Kansas City, USA
Senior Research Fellow in Theology,
Nazarene Theological College, Manchester, UK

When I think of God's man, I give thought to a particular outstanding man, a specific man who might have made heroic news today, and a man who is standing strong through the trials of his tomorrows. I think of none other than Dr. Samuel W. Hynd. The scripture that comes to my mind is Proverbs 2:20. "Walk in the way of good men, and keep the paths of the righteous."

I have known Dr. Samuel for 15 years. He is most sincere in his walk with our Lord Jesus. I would describe him as being a personal friend to our Heavenly Father. His sensitivity to the poor, sick, and needy has been obvious to all who know him. He has lived a life best described in Psalm 112:9, "He shall be exalted with honour." His days have been filled with loving kindness to the rejected. His profession as a medical doctor revealed his acceptance of all who came to him. He has spent decades faithfully obeying his call as a missionary doctor to the sick, the diseased, and the HIV/AIDS patient who faces imminent death. Dr. Samuel sincerely lived his life in giving help to the poor, the needy, the widow, and the orphan.

This book will renew your vision and rekindle lively hope within your spirit. Throughout the pages of this book, you will learn how the Hynd Family through faithfulness and obedience to their calling brought the Gospel, education, and medicine into the Nation of Swaziland. Their lives of service to the King of kings and Lord of lords and their respect and honor for their homeland and country of Swaziland is a true story that will inspire you.

Through the pages of this book you will laugh, weep, and rejoice as you read and learn of this one man, Dr. Samuel Hynd, who faithfully lived his days to help meet the needs of the poor, the sick, the orphans, the widows, and the needy. Through all the years his life he has displayed heartfelt compassion. He displayed understanding with wisdom and he gave instruction to those who were hopeless. I can say with all sincerity that your life will be changed and your vision will grow stronger as you read this outstanding story of Dr. Samuel Hynd's service to the Swazi Nation.

He has displayed respect and honor to the leaders of the Nation. I believe that when he stands before the Almighty to give an account for the deeds that he has done in this life that a proclamation from Heaven will echo, "Well done thou good and faithful servant. You have fought a good fight. You have kept the faith. Enter into your heavenly home." This book is intended to encourage you, the reader, to be faithful in the thing that excites you the most spiritually and to proclaim that you can be all that God has inspired and called you to be. Please allow the pages of this book to awaken your calling.

In loving service to my Swazi Family and to those faithful called of God people within the Swazi Nation.

June McKinney
End-Time Harvesters for the Nations, Inc.
Jacksonville, Florida, USA
Co Director with Elizabeth Hynd
New Hope Center, Swaziland, Africa

FOOTPRINTS
ON AFRICAN
HEARTS
AND LANDS

Footprints on African Hearts and Lands: The Life and Work of Dr. Samuel W. Hynd

© 2014 by Gwen Ellis with Elizabeth Hynd
ISBN-13: 9780988825697
Published by Seaside Creative Services
Nashville, Tennessee
All rights reserved.

Scripture taken from the *Holy Bible, New International Version®,* NIV® Copyright © 1973, 1978, 1984, 2011 by Biblica, Inc.® Used by permission. All rights reserved worldwide. Also taken from the King James Version (KJV), public domain.

Certain phrases, punctuation, and capitalization are traditional to Swazi customs and not at the discretion of the writers and editors.

DEDICATION

Dr. Samuel and I (Gwen Ellis) discussed to whom we would dedicate this book. Dr. Samuel would like to dedicate it to the young generation that holds the world's destiny and future in their hands. It is a fitting tribute for him to make as he has devoted the entirety of his life to helping and preserving generations of Swazi people.

So, to the youth of the Swaziland, we dedicate this book and pray that you will pick up the torch of truth and service and carry on until our Lord returns to take us all home.

HIS FAMILY CREST
THE ROSE CLAN COAT OF ARMS
OF THE HYND FAMILY HERITAGE

The Rose Family Crest consists of the words
"Constant and True," a Belt of Truth, and a Harp of Praise.
Conifer evergreen trees represent Jesus' death on Calvary's
tree and resurrection unto everlasting life.

"Brothers and sisters, think of what you were when you were called.
Not many of you were wise by human standards; not many were
influential; not many were of noble birth. But God chose the foolish
things of the world to shame the wise; God chose the weak things of the
world to shame the strong. God chose the lowly things of this world
and the despised things—and the things that are not—to nullify the
things that are, so that no one may boast before him."
1 Corinthians 1:26-29, NIV

CONTENTS

ACKNOWLEDGEMENTS

It takes many people to capture the story of a life. I want to thank *Babe* (Father) Hynd—the good and beloved doctor himself—for the hours and hours we spent together discussing the mountain of information and stories of his life. I will never forget a time when we were discussing certain conditions now existing in the world and he asked, "Where are the preachers? Where are the men of God? Why don't they do something?" Why, indeed?

I want to thank his oldest daughter Elizabeth for providing the bones of the book. She spent endless hours interviewing, remembering, questioning, and clarifying with her father before I took up the writing.

I want to thank his administrative assistant, Mandla Dlamini, for transporting me between New Hope Centre and Dr. Hynd's cottage on Elwandle Road, for printing out endless versions of the document, and for tracking down papers, articles, and information we needed.

Thanks, too, to the ladies, Dudu Ginindza and Nokuthula Lukhele, who carried many cups of coffee and tea and lunches and dinners to us while we worked and served them graciously on trays. We barely looked up, but we were grateful.

Thank you, Annie Cheung, for all the photos you scanned and organized and made sure arrived in my email. You are a priceless jewel.

Thanks to Thami Ncube who gave us a tour through the ACTS II clinic and answered a host of questions our group had about HIV/AIDS and the care and treatment of those who have it. Thanks also for his endless devotion to these people.

Thanks belong to my two children who have given so much of their time: Wendy Weising, for copyediting the book; and Mark Weising, for doing the typesetting. Thanks also to my friend Barbara Scott, who wanted to copyedit the book without charge but found it could not fit into her schedule.

A big thanks goes to Rob Williams, our brilliant designer, for the cover. Rob, you just never miss. Thanks.

And above all, I want to thank my Lord and Savior for choosing me to tell this story. I will never be the same because of what I learned sitting at the feet of Dr. Samuel Wilson Hynd.

FOREWORD

There are some moments in life that you never forget. Meeting Dr. Samuel Hynd for the first time was one of those moments for me.

After learning that Swaziland had the highest HIV/AIDS adult prevalence rate in the world and that each year thousands of children were being orphaned and left to try to survive on their own, I was convinced that the Lord impressed a vision on my heart. I preached a sermon to my local congregation challenging them to respond. That sermon became the launching point for a church-wide vision to establish a partnership with the Swazi church in response to the AIDS crisis. We organized an exploratory trip to Swaziland to determine our next steps forward. Within months, I was standing in a hotel lobby in Manzini, Swaziland, when someone tapped me on the shoulder and said, "So you are the one." I turned to be introduced to Dr. Hynd and his daughter, Elizabeth. I soon learned that someone from Swaziland had been in that worship service a few months earlier, when I had shared the Swaziland vision. That person had purchased a CD of the sermon and brought it back to Dr. Hynd, saying, "You need to listen to this." He did. In fact, as he later told me, he listened to it over and over again. He began to tell everyone in Swaziland that there was a pastor in the United States who understood what was happening in his country.

I tell that portion of the story to underscore how the providence of God brought our friendship together. I could never have known that God would arrange for someone, who had never attended our church before, to be present on that particular Sunday and for that person to hear my unusual sermon. I could never have known that God would put that sermon into the hands of one of the most influential, spiritual leaders in the Kingdom of Swaziland. I could never have known how many open doors Dr. Hynd's endorsement and support would bring to what has become the Swaziland Partnership.

Having faithfully given of themselves to the present and future good of the country, the Hynds are a revered household name in Swaziland. Dr. Samuel Hynd is a Swazi at heart. He has served in some of the Nation's highest offices. He is known not only for his medical expertise—decades of his life were spent leading the medical team of Raleigh Fitkin Memorial Nazarene Hospital in Manzini before becoming the Minister of Health for the country—but also for his profound commitment to bring spiritual wholeness to the brokenness of the Nation.

Dr. Hynd is now ninety and is officially "retired" from his capacity at the hospital, but he still spends time at his AIDS health clinic. (He once told me, "Some people retire; some people re-fire!") His daughter, Audrey, reports, "There are days when Dad is really tired and wants to rest. But then he sees the lines of HIV/AIDS patients, many of them having waited all day or even overnight to see him, and he knows he must continue on." The clinic is the culmination of his lifelong dream.

Dr. Hynd often recalls that the mission strategy of the early Nazarene missionaries in Swaziland was to pattern themselves after Jesus' ministry to preach, teach, and heal. I personally know of no one who has incarnated that ministry of compassion more profoundly than Dr. Samuel Hynd.

He is a friend, mentor, and patriarch. It is my honor to recommend his life's story to you.

David A. Busic
General Superintendent, Church of the Nazarene
Lent 2014

INTRODUCTION

The van full of volunteers left the highway, drove through the gate, and rolled to a stop outside the new AIDS clinic in Manzini, Swaziland. The thin winter sun on this July day barely took the chill off the air. Visible in the distance was a kind of town made up of miserable-looking hovels. Could it be that people actually lived there?

As volunteers climbed out of the van, a door onto the wide veranda of the clinic opened and there he stood: Dr. Samuel Hynd, veteran missionary doctor extraordinaire. The wind tousled *Dokotela* (doctor) Samuel's white hair as he crossed the veranda and walked slowly and deliberately down the steps, his worn navy blue blazer flapping in the wind as he approached.

"Welcome, welcome," he said with a decidedly British accent. "Come in and see what we have here." We went up the steps to the veranda and waited there a few minutes for other staff to join us for a short introduction to what we were about to see inside the brand new clinic. On the veranda were some obviously very sick people who were awaiting treatment. The inside revealed a reception area, treatment rooms, offices, and a consultation area where the team sat to hear the story of how the clinic came to be.

Dr. Samuel Hynd, at the time, was eighty-seven and had just recently closed his medical practice in the Manzini city centre to found this clinic. Well past the age when most people retire, here he was realizing a dream of a clinic to treat the thousands upon thousands of Swazis infected with the HIV/AIDS virus. He began to tell us the story—a story that started long before he was born—about his father, Dr. David Hynd, hearing God's strong and sure call to meet the needs of the Swazi people in Swaziland.

1

A NEW NATION

The story of Dr. Samuel Wilson Hynd's amazing life began long before the infant baby boy first opened his eyes in Scotland. The story started when his father, Dr. David Hynd, heard the call of God that changed the direction of his life and sent him to meet the needs of the people of Swaziland. But before this part of the story began, generations before either of the Hynds lived, a young King Somhlolo (Sobhuza I) pulled together a number of tribes to form the Nation of Swaziland. King Somhlolo is considered to be the "father" of the Swazi Nation.

Swaziland was a Kingdom of Nguni people, part of the Bantu nations, who, before the sixteenth century, migrated southward from the mountains of Ethiopia through Uganda and Kenya and along the coastal region of Mozambique in search of grazing ground for their herds of cattle. They reached a major river gorge in the Ubombo Mountain Range and turned inland to settle peacefully in the hills and valleys to the west of the Ubombo Range. Settling first in what is now northern Zululand in about 1750, they gradually moved northward in the 1800s to establish themselves in what was to become modern day Swaziland.

Initially, the people were composed of a number of clans or families until King Somhlolo brought unity to the clans and formed a Nation of peace-loving, beautiful people who became known as the Swazis, which included the Dlaminis, Ndwandwes, Mtetwas, Mabuzas, Shongwes, Mkatschwas, Nxumalos, and others.

The Nation of Swaziland is unique in that God visited the founding King Somhlolo in a vision. Somhlolo's very name means "the one who astounded or amazed us," and this is due to the fact that when he was born he was still enclosed in the embryonic sac and should have died, but by the grace and purpose of God, he was saved by the traditional healer-physician, who cut the embryonic sac and released the founding King of the Nation of the Swazis. Later, as this man grew up tending His father's cattle and goats, he learned to hear the voice of *Simakadze* (the Almighty God).

As an old man, His Majesty had a vision . . . a dream or a visitation from Heaven. He was visited by the Lord Jesus Christ who stood before him and told him of a people coming to the land who had pointed noses and long, straight, horsetail-like hair. These people would be carrying two things: a

Somhlolo Rock on Bethany Mountain

Book, or *Umculu*, in their right hand (the hand of honor) and a coin or button, an *indilinga or indingiliza*, in the left hand (the hand of dishonor). The King asked in His dream what He should do. The Lord told King Somhlolo never to shed the blood of these people of the pointed noses and horsetail-like hair. He was to take the *Umculu*, the Book, and "eat it on the inside," and His Nation would live. The Lord further said to ignore the coin or button, which represented money. This vision has been the guiding principle for the establishment of this Nation, its foreign affairs and policies, and the peaceful resolution of challenges and problems.

The King awakened in the morning and called the Nation together to inform them of His heavenly visitation. Sobhuza's (Somhlolo's) people listened carefully to His words and have tried ever since to observe the advice of listening to those who brought the Bible, even though they have found it impossible to avoid the *indingiliza*—the coin. The people of Sobhuza have tried ever since and at all costs not to shed white men's blood in their land.

On this point, author George Frame makes an interesting observation:

> The Swazis were one of the few powerful Bantu tribes whose relations with the Europeans did not lead them into war. This was partly owing to a powerful tradition against fighting the white man, which began with Sobhuza I at the turn of the nineteenth century and was subscribed to by his successor Mswati. The tradition was almost mystical in its origin but its survival had much to do with an intelligent respect for the white man's superior military strength. . . . As they never fought the European, and the Swazi was never conquered by him.[1]

It was not long thereafter that the King died and went on to be with His ancestors. A descendant of King Somhlolo heard that a people of pointed noses and long, horsetail-like hair who carried "the Book" were in Greytown, South Africa, to the south of Swaziland. This King immediately sent men to collect the *Umculu*, "the Book," and bring it, along with some teachers of the Book, to show the Swazi people how to "eat the

Book on the inside." The warriors he sent found the Methodist missionaries in conference. The warriors had to wait for the adjournment of the conference before they could present the request of His Majesty.

When the Methodists concluded their conference, their response was that Swaziland was not yet on their agenda. The warriors, however, refused to return unsuccessful to their King. They said they would stay until such time as the Methodists could come and share the *Umculu* with the King and His people. The conference then resolved to send Reverend Alison and two Basuto evangelists to Swaziland. The Swazis accompanied these men back to the Orange Free State, as it was called at the time, to a town called Thaba N'Chu, where Alison and the evangelists collected their belongings. They began the long journey on horseback to meet His Majesty at Mbangweni, His Royal Residence in the south of Swaziland. His Majesty received them with great joy, then gave them a mountain called Mahamba to use as their home base with the commission to teach the Swazi Nation how to "eat the Word of God on the inside that the Nation may live," as the Lord had spoken in the prophecy.

King Somhlolo's vision and his descendants' determination to find the *Umculu* set the tone for the Swazi Nation, causing the Nation ever to turn toward God Almighty in politics, religion, and relationships with other nations. In the writings of A.F. Gardiner in *A History of Swaziland*, he writes of an encounter he had with men from Sobhuza I's (Somhlolo's) tribe.

He learned that the people of Sobhuza I had never seen white-skinned people, although they had heard about them through Sobhuza's vision. They also told him that the Swazis worshipped a supreme being known in their language as *Mvelamchanti* or *Mlentengamunye*, who had created everything and who expected everyone to lead a good life. Gardiner invited the three into his hut so he could tell them about his God.

At the turn of the twentieth century, the Afrikaner Boers (farmers) and the British were at war over land in Southern Africa. White people were fighting one another, and the young

King of Swaziland, Sobhuza II, great-great-great-grandson of King Somhlolo, was concerned that the warfare would bring bloodshed and chaos into his small Kingdom. The Swazi Nation had never known war or bloodshed, as they were a peaceful people whose tradition was to resolve matters through negotiation and dialogue, not through might and destruction. The warlike behavior of the white foreigners was not acceptable in their land.

In 1890, South Africa took sovereignty over Swaziland but never established full power. After the Second Boer War (1899-1902), King Sobhuza II saw that the wars and land grabs that were going on at the time could destroy His country. So with great wisdom, the King and His council of elders decided to go to England and consult with Queen Victoria about how to maintain peace in their country.

His Majesty and His council embarked on the long journey over land and sea to London, England, where He met with Her Majesty Queen Victoria. An agreement was signed between the sovereign monarch of the United Kingdom and the sovereign monarch of Swaziland that made the Kingdom of Swaziland a Protectorate of the British Empire. A British presence was established in Swaziland with a British High Commissioner and a small number of officials. Since no nation can be ruled by two monarchs, and King Sobhuza II had asked Queen Victoria for help which she willingly gave, He humbly and graciously stepped down from being King of Swaziland and took the title of Paramount Chief.

Thus it was that when Dr. David Hynd and his young family arrived in Swaziland, it was a Protectorate with a British High Commissioner in residence in Bremersdorp. (The *dorp*, or town, of Bremer had been established by a Jewish man who first started a general store to host the mail stagecoach service. Later, at the time of independence, Bremersdorp became Manzini, named after a chief. Manzini means "water.")

The British High Commissioner's residence was located on the hill above a small collection of shops and houses that constituted the town of Bremersdorp. As a child, Dr. Samuel played there with the Commissioner's children. Later on, the High Commission was relocated to the capital city of Mbabane, and the house was converted into a commercial hotel (the George Hotel), which still stands and operates as the main hotel of the city today.

Before the young Samuel ever played at the Commissioner's house, a great deal of history had taken place to blaze the trail for the Hynd family's work. Through sweat and toil, early missionaries had faithfully laid the groundwork for what was to become the Hynd family's legacy to Swaziland.

Note

1. George Frame, *Blood Brother of the Swazis: The life story of David Hynd*, (Beacon Hill Press, Printed Book No Copyright Digital Edition 03/28/98 By Holiness Data Ministry).

2

EARLY
MISSIONARIES

One hundred years ago, Harmon Schmelzenbach, a young American man from Oklahoma, read the story of Dr. David Livingstone, renowned missionary doctor and abolisher of the slave trade in Africa. Afterward, the Spirit of God led him to Africa. He completed his studies in theology and took a steamer ship from the United States to Cape Town, South Africa. There, the Spirit of God led him to meet and marry the love of his life, Lulu. They bought four donkeys and a wagon.

On October 3, 1910, the young Schmelzenbach family climbed into their wagon and started on the long and treacherous trip north through the mountains of Zululand and into Swaziland. Schmelzenbach felt called to an area in Swaziland where no white missionaries had ever been allowed to go: the gold mining town of Piggs Peak in the northern mountains of Swaziland near the place where the Swazi Queen Mother resided.

In time, Schmelzenbach or *Sibaha*, as he was known in Swaziland, arrived at his destination of Piggs Peak and began preaching the Word of God and the message of salvation. He was taken to meet the Queen Mother. She welcomed him to join the other missionaries who had been invited by King Mswati I in 1854. She gave him land at a place called Endzingeni, not far from Piggs Peak. This was in the healthier, cooler area of Swaziland, above the level where malaria and typhoid infested the land.

The Schmelzenbachs built a small stone church and either walked or travelled on horseback or mule to visit the homesteads and share the Word of God, bringing the good news that Jesus died to give them abundant life. However, the local witch doctors warned the people that if they listened to the missionaries, they would be cursed. The people became afraid of Harmon Schmelzenbach and his family.

Endzingeni Tabernacle, replacing Schmelzenbach's first stone church, which they soon outgrew at Endzingeni Nazarene Mission.

After a year, the Swazi Queen Mother granted the Schmelzenbachs more land where they could build a mission. It was within the jurisdiction of the Queen Mother's powers to distribute and allocate land among the people. Soon a group of African soldiers approached Her Majesty about allowing them to push the Schmelzenbachs off the land or perhaps even kill them. For reasons explainable only by divine providence, Her Majesty told the soldiers they could do nothing to harm the missionaries.

Schmelzenbach had begun the work, but he had a tremendous need for a medical team to come to Swaziland. He was a preacher who knew little about medicine. People all over the country were dying from malaria, typhoid, smallpox, and dysentery. The best he could do was to ride a mule out into the bush and deliver quinine tablets to those affected by malaria. Some of the people began to respond to his primitive medical treatment. However, more than quinine was needed; these people needed extensive medical care.

Besides illness, there were accidents—horrible ones whose victims required medical attention. Schmelzenbach could do little or nothing to help. For example, an ox attacked a young boy and ripped open his stomach with its horns, and all the child's intestines spilled out. His parents went to a witchdoctor who turned them away because he couldn't help them. He advised them to go try the Schmelzenbachs. The parents covered the boy with a cloth sack and put him on a sledge. An ox dragged the sledge—a device made from the fork of a tree stump used for plowing—up to the mountain mission station. Preacher Schmelzenbach and his wife came out to see what had happened to the boy. When they saw the boy's condition, they wondered what a preacher should do in this situation.

Mrs. Schmelzenbach was a resourceful woman. She found her sewing bag, took out a needle and thread, and while people held the boy down, she pushed his intestines back inside his body and stitched up his abdomen. Then they held hands and prayed over the boy that God would preserve his life and heal him. What she did was against all the rules and regulations of medicine. She had no medical background or knowledge; she just stitched. There also was no hygiene, no cleanliness, no disinfectants, and no antibiotics. The boy should have died, but he didn't. He survived and stayed at the mission. Eventually he became a preacher.

When you are dying and someone comes to your rescue, you are ready to listen to what he has to say. So Schmelzenbach not only saved their physical lives but also saved their souls.

While he was successful at leading people to Christ, he knew he wasn't doing enough. He wrote again to the headquarters of the Church of the Nazarene in Kansas City, Missouri, in America, begging for a medical team. He continued writing and asking the church leadership to send medical doctors and staff for the good of the people.

The Schmelzenbach family remained faithful to the call God had placed upon their lives. Through their faithfulness, many people in Swaziland came to know Christ and then took the Word of God and taught their own people. Perseverance, determination, and trust in God were, at times, the only things that kept the Schmelzenbach family in Swaziland. On May 22, 1929, Harmon Schmelzenbach died among the people that he had served. After his death, the men and women of Africa continued to love and honor him as a special man of God.

3

DR. DAVID HYND

World War I ended, leaving nations bereft of young men and families bereft of sons and fathers. Many children lost all the men in their lives, which meant no dads, no brothers, and no granddads. The bloodshed over the hills and valleys of Europe changed the history of the world. Warfare had become a killing game par excellence. The war was long and *intense,* but after a while, the Allies prevailed and brought an end to the war and to the slaughter.

When World War I ended, David Hynd returned from battle to his home in Scotland. Though a survivor, he was shattered by the destruction and death he had witnessed. He

Hynd family children: David, Kate, and John as children

wondered why he had returned when thousands upon thousands of others had not. He began to seek God, asking why he was alive when so many of his comrades had died. He asked the Almighty for the reason why he had been preserved.

One day, not long after this prayer, while reading the newspaper, the Holy Ghost stirred his heart. He read a tiny news clipping about a small British protectorate in the southeastern part of Africa that had no health care for its people. They were dying of malaria, typhoid, bilharzia, and dysentery—all treatable diseases in the post-World War I era. The southeastern African country in the news that day was the Kingdom of Swaziland—a tiny country nestled peacefully in the mountains between Mozambique (then known as Portuguese East Africa) and two other provinces (then known as the Transvaal and Natal, which later became part of South Africa).

As Swaziland was a British protectorate, one would have thought that there would be medical facilities and education for the national people. But there were no hospitals and no schools for the common folk. The British government had built a hospital in the capital of Mbabane, to the north, and in Hlatikhulu, to the south, but these hospitals served only government employees and their families. David Hynd was immediately concerned that in a world with medical remedies for the diseases infecting Africans, people were dying needlessly.

With the Holy Spirit guiding him, David immediately contacted government officials in London to enquire as to how this could be the situation in a country under British protection. The British government informed him of what he already knew: that it only made health-care services available in its protectorates for government employees.

David offered his services to the Commonwealth Officer to correct this act of negligence on behalf of his own government. The Foreign Office, rather than throwing him out the door, arranged for David, who was a lecturer of mathematics and logic at the University of Glasgow, Scotland, to be retrained with a degree in medicine at the same university and then arranged for him to specialize in tropical diseases at the Royal College of Tropical Medicine and Hygiene in London.

*   *   *

During this time, David met Kanema Agnes Sharpe, the daughter of a renowned Scottish Christian leader, Reverend Dr. George Sharpe. Sharpe had been a minister of a Congregational Church in Glasgow, Scotland, but had been thrown out of the denomination for his teachings on the Holy Spirit's role in the life of the believer. He believed that the Holy Spirit empowered an individual to live a holy life as a Christian.

Undeterred, Reverend Sharpe moved with those in the congregation who believed as he did, across the street to a beer hall on Burgher Street in Parkhead, Scotland. They founded a new church called the Parkhead Pentecostal Church in 1906, but in 1909, as he reached out to other fellowships around the United Kingdom who had similarly left the mainstream church; his fledgling congregation formed a denomination called the Pentecostal Church of Scotland.

Rev. George Sharpe moved from the Parkhead Congregational Church to a beer hall across the road.

In time, his congregation grew, and he continued to reach out to other fellowships around the United Kingdom. These small gatherings of people were prayer groups, fellowships, or small churches. They were committed to the knowledge of God's plan for our redemption through the death and resurrection of the Son of God, Jesus Christ, and the fullness of the Holy Spirit.

Rev. George Sharpe's first building on Burgher Street, Glasgow, Scotland, was built in 1906.

Sharpe believed it was the way God had intended for us to live. Later, in 1915, he amalgamated the fledgling denomination in the United Kingdom with a similar movement in the United States, which had met some time before at Pilot Point, Texas, to form the Pentecostal Church of the Nazarene. Later in 1919, the denomination was renamed the Church of the Nazarene.

David and Kanema were both teaching at the University of Glasgow—she being a theologian and he being a mathematician and logician. They were married in 1918 in the Parkhead Church of Scotland and started their young family with the birth of their first child, Isabel Grace, on 20 September 1919, and their second child, the subject of this book, Samuel Wilson, born on 18 December 1924.

Sometime earlier Pastor Sharpe had met Harmon Schmelzenbach and his wife, Lulu. He was intrigued by the stories they told about Swaziland and stunned by the great medical needs there. Their report of the need for medical help was just as real as the need for spiritual help and that they were helpless in the face of such need touched the hearts of David and Kanema. They were led by the Spirit of God to go to Swaziland, primarily because of the needs described by Harmon and his wife.

Dr. Samuel Hynd at the home of his grandparents at 33 Muiryfauld Drive, where he was born in an upstairs room on 18 December 1924.

So it was that when Samuel was five weeks old, the family's journey to a new life in the land of Africa began. The four of them boarded the train from Glasgow to Carlisle where they would say farewell to Dr. David's parents, the Samuel Wilson Hynds. Young Samuel had been named after his grandfather, Samuel.

The family then proceeded by train to London and then on another train to Southampton, where they boarded the Arundal Castle, an ocean liner bound for Cape Town, South Africa. They had all of their earthly belongings with them.

Traveling with the young family were Kanema's parents, the Reverend George and Jane Brayton Rose Sharpe and their daughter, Isabel Rose. By this time, Reverend Sharpe had been appointed missions superintendent of the Church of the Nazarene, overseeing the missions work of the Church in China, India, the Middle East, and Africa, so he and his wife had come along to see firsthand the needs Schmel-zenbach had related.

Samuel Wilson Hynd and wife, Jane, (the grandparents of Dr. Samuel) with their four children: Kathryn, Grace, John, and David.

The entourage sailed for seventeen days on the Atlantic Ocean arriving in Cape Town on 9 June 1925. Dr. David, unable to sleep because of his excitement, was up at 2:30 AM gazing out at the watery horizon to catch a first glimpse of Sub-Saharan Africa, where he would be working for the rest of his days. Table Mountain, looming above Cape Town, came into view through a hazy mist. This was it. This was Africa. This was the continent of his calling. Before disembarking the ship, Dr. Hynd and his family knelt down once more and recommitted themselves to their calling.

From Cape Town, the Hynd family took a train across the expansive Karoo Desert (elevation of 5,751 feet) and up to the city of Johannesburg in the Witwatersrand Ridge of mountains. In Johannesburg, they purchased a car (an open Dodge vehicle) and began the drive to Swaziland. Travel by road was the only way into the tiny Kingdom. It took three days of hard driving to reach their destination. They had to follow the railway line across farmland, and as they crossed each farm, they had to jump out of the car to open and close the fence gate, making progress slow and tedious. They drove through rivers that soaked their luggage, making it necessary when they stopped to rest at night, to spread everything out to dry. One time the car sank up to its axles in a mud hole and only got out with the help of two women, one carrying a tiny baby tied on her back. Later they were swamped in a bog and had to be rescued by a team of four oxen.

When they rounded the bend from the Highveld of the Transvaal, they found themselves on the border of the country they would call home for the rest of their lives. Here they would live and here they would die and be buried. Instead of the strange land they had expected, they saw a scene that vividly reminded them of their native Scotland. Rolled out before their view were the mountains of Swaziland so like the Scottish Highlands.

It was evening when they arrived at the hilltop where the building that was intended as their "home" was located. What they found there shocked them beyond belief. The building looked like a skeleton of a house. There were no windows or doors. Even more shocking was the fact that the house had no roof. They could not bring their young daughter and infant son to live in a house with only partial walls and no roof. There was nothing to do but drive on to the nearest mission station in Stegi (now Siteki), forty miles further on. By now night had fallen, and the family drove in utter darkness toward the home of Reverend and Mrs. Shirley, who were also missionaries in Swaziland. A Miss Murtle Pelley also lived at the mission station. The Shirleys and Miss Pelley warmly welcomed the exhausted travelers.

The next morning, Dr. David awoke with a raging fever. Miss Pelley, a missionary nurse, diagnosed his illness as typhoid fever. The group carried him into her dispensary where he lay desperately ill for seven days. Since he was not improving, it was decided he must go to the Swiss Mission Hospital in Lourenzo Marques (modern day Maputo) in Mozambique (then known as Portuguese East Africa). Dr. David rode in the back of the car for seventy miles of tortuous conditions that would put a strain even on a healthy person.

He lay in the hospital for nine days and, during that time, questioned why God had brought him to Swaziland if he was to die upon arrival. Why should his first experience of medicine in Swaziland be as that of a patient and not as a doctor? The experience became a defining moment in his life. After recovering his strength, he wrote home:

> Although I have come through very deep waters since I left you all in the comforts of home, and have experienced much that has tested my faith and obedience to the very utmost, yet I do praise Him that today He is sweeter than ever before and my only desire is to spend myself and my all in the great and glorious privilege of pointing lost souls to their Savior. We cannot be great sympathizers until we have been great sufferers. I pray that my own experience of suffering will have prepared me to minister to the indescribable sufferings of the neglected masses around me.[1]

Only a week after Dr. David was released from the hospital, he left Stegi for a missionary council meeting at Peniel, a mission station in the north near the mining town of Piggs Peak. Mrs. Shirley, Miss Pelley, Kanema Hynd, and the Hynd children rode in a spring-less wagon drawn by sixteen oxen. Dr. Hynd and Reverend Shirley walked alongside the wagon.

The two men had to wade fully clothed through waist-deep rivers. Big John, a Swazi evangelist, carried the women and children across these rivers on his broad shoulders, to lighten the wagon's load so that it would not be bogged down in the river. At night they slept out on the Bushveld under the expansive and star-filled southern hemisphere sky.

As they went along, word travelled ahead of them that a *dokotela* was passing that way. Many sick were brought to him along the trail. Others pled with him to turn aside to a *kraal* (the grass and wood frame huts of a homestead) where someone lay sick or dying. This was why he had trained as a medical doctor, and this was why he had come.[2]

*   *   *

Soon David met with the British High Commissioner. The Commissioner arranged for him to meet with the Queen Mother, who acted as regent for her young son, King Sobhuza II. When She heard Dr. David's heart for the *EmaSwati* (the Swazi people) and his passionate desire to bring an end to the loss of lives by using medicine for treatable disease. The Queen Mother asked if he would consider establishing his hospital centrally in the country rather than in the mountains to the north where previous plans had been made for a Nazarene hospital. She asked this because the Swazi people had predominantly settled in the rolling, grassy hills of the Middleveld and not in the chilly, rugged mountain areas of the Highveld. The Swazi people had found the Middleveld was warmer and had good, arable land for grazing and farming, so the concentration of the population was there.

The British government, the Queen Mother, and the young King Sobhuza II first identified a location for the hospital in the lower lying area next to the town of Bremersdorp. The Mzimnene River near this place was infested with mosquitoes and bilharzia organisms. (Bilharzia is a disease that affects the kidneys, bladder, and even the liver. It is caused by a parasite that lives in snails in the warm river waters of the tropics.)

David Hynd was advised by the Swazi evangelists that the hospital should be established on a small hilltop near Bremersdorp rather than next to the river. All parties thought about it and agreed that the higher place away from the river, with its infestation of malaria mosquitoes and bilharzia, would be the safer place to put the hospital.

On a sunny, windy day, Dr. David Hynd, his young wife, Kanema, his father-in-law, George Sharpe, George's wife, Jane, their daughter, Isabel Rose, David's four-year-old daughter, Isabel Grace, and Samuel, who was still crawling, knelt on the grassy hilltop—the future site of the hospital—and gave thanks to God that He had brought them all the way from Glasgow, Scotland, to meet the needs of the Swazi people. They dedicated the land and the care of these people into God's all loving hands.

Notes
  1. Ibid.
  2. Ibid.

4

PUTTING DOWN ROOTS

The Hynds first set about to build a mud and stone family home on the hilltop. The house had a front veranda, which would become the first church, clinic, and surgery for the Swazi people. It also had a living room with a big fireplace in the corner and three small bedrooms for the family. On the back of the house was another patio that served as both kitchen and laundry, and which was to become the first schoolroom.

The first David Hynd family home built on the hilltop in 1926. It served as home, church, clinic, and school in the early days.

Once the home was built, Dr. David would ride his horse out to visit surrounding homesteads. Often he took little Samuel with him. His purpose for these visits was to make friends and to see if there was anyone who was sick and needed help. Initially, people were very wary of these white folks, but in time, David Hynd was named *Thandabantu*, which means "Lover of People."

The first stone house built on grassy hilltop in Swaziland. The front portion was an open verandah used for the surgery and also for church services in 1926, but in 2006 it became the consulting area for VCT (Voluntary Counseling and Testing) for HIV/AIDS.

As soon as the family moved into the stone house, they learned that the local shops would send a donkey-pulled wagon from Mr. Bremer's shop down by the river to deliver orders. The two young deliverymen begged Samuel's mother to help them learn to read, as they could not read the orders they took. She began "school" on the dirt floor of the kitchen of the stone house. There was no furniture, so the young men brought wood-slat crates that were used to deliver the barrels of paraffin (kerosene) everyone burned in their lamps, as there was no electricity.

The kitchen area of the first stone house, which served as the family's kitchen and laundry.
It was also the very first classroom where Kanema Hynd began to teach literacy.
It now serves as part of HIV/AIDS testing services.

The classes were held in the evenings after the students had finished their work at the store for the day. The class started with three young men using stone slate tablets to learn their ABCs. Then a few other young boys joined the class. Then the sons of farmers whose fathers required them to tend the goats and cattle during the day came at night too. Families all around the Bremersdorp/Manzini region began to see the value of their children learning to read and write. They saw how it helped them in their work and in getting jobs in the slowly blossoming town. So they too began sending their boys to night school in the kitchen. Slowly, the class grew and filled the kitchen.

In addition to the school, Dr. David and Kanema began services on the front veranda of their house. Dr. David continued going on horseback to visit the surrounding neighbors in their homesteads.

In 1913, Kanema's mother had been the second woman to become an ordained minister in the United Kingdom. She passed on her passion and vision to her daughter and Kanema

followed in her mother's footsteps and was the third woman
to be ordained in the United Kingdom. Kanema had always
been a woman of vision and the next step in her vision was to
build a stone church. She wanted to build a church that was
enormous by the standards of those days. Now with her
kitchen overflowing and the veranda packed with church at-
tenders, she decided that the church had to be built right away.
The new church building could also serve as a school.

The Old Stone Church as it is now. The church is waiting for renovation as funds are being
raised. It will then serve as a historical museum for the work of the Church of the Nazarene
in Swaziland. It was the first church and school in Manzini (Bremersdorp).

Most churches in Scotland were built of stones so that was
what the Hynds planned for Swaziland. However, Dr. David
did not have enough funds to build such a building. Even
though he had not been in Swaziland very long, he had developed a good friendship with His Majesty King Sobhuza II. He
went to His Majesty for permission to gather stones from the
mountain across the valley to build the church. The King agreed.

By this time Samuel was a little boy and he delighted in going to bring stones for the church. He said, "I remember riding

in the wagon drawn by sixteen oxen across the land to the valley where we then had to change the oxen because the next mountain was a restricted area due to an outbreak of foot-and-mouth disease. We could not take our oxen in there. So, a bunch of the young men and boys accompanied the wagon, changed the oxen, and then went on with the wagon up the hill on the other side to collect stones and load them on the wagon and bring them back down the valley. Then they had to change the oxen again and pull the stones up to the top of the hill, where they deposited the ever-expanding collection of stones to build the church."

The Old Stone Church belfry. The bell was smelted in Blantyre, Scotland, and shipped to Cape Town, then over land by train to Johannesburg and was later transported by ox wagon down the Escarpment to Bremersdorp.It was the only imported item in the entire building and it still hangs in the belfry today. When a long metal wire is pulled the resounding peels of announcement and invitation ring out.

Once the building was completed, the Old Stone Church became a hive of activity during the week. It functioned all week as a school. Afternoon women's meetings were also held there. On Sunday mornings, the church bell would ring out over the hills and valleys gathering people to come and worship. Soon the sound of praise from the resonating, powerful voices of the Swazis would be heard over the hills and across into Bremersdorp.

The church and the school on the Hynd's veranda did outgrow the space, and just as the kitchen school was bursting its seams, Kanema was able to move it to the Stone Church. The new school was an open-plan classroom with different levels of learning in each corner of the auditorium. As there were no schools in Swaziland, there were also no Swazi teachers. So, Kanema recruited some teachers from Zimbabwe and

South Africa. Then she set about educating the Swazi children in earnest.

*   *   *

Soon it was time for little Isabel to begin school. Her parents enrolled her in the Bremersdorp Government Primary School for government officials' children and the other expatriate children in town. The school was one-and-a-half miles (3 km) away from their home. To get her to the school, one of the Swazi workers would carry her there on his shoulders.

The family had brought no toys from Scotland for their children, so while Isabel went to school, Samuel spent his days playing with the other Swazi children in the dirt, making clay animals, building roads, and creating mud houses that represented homes, schools, clinics, churches, and warehouses. He earned himself the nickname *S'tolobane*, meaning "the small town maker."

He also played with the Swazi neighborhood children, climbing trees and even building a wooden go-kart-like vehicle for speeding around the hilltop. He learned the SiSwati language and became more fluent in it than he was in English. When he was the right age, he began attending school with his sister in Bremersdorp.

*   *   *

It was at about this time that Mrs. Fitkin, a strong missionary-minded woman, who was the president of the Nazarene Women's Missionary Society in the United States (later known as the Nazarene World Missions Society- NWMS), heard about the work being done in Swaziland and the need for medical workers. The Fitkins had a son named Raleigh who heard about the many sick and dying people in Swaziland. He wanted to become a doctor and go out to Africa to help them. Unfortunately, the boy became ill and died from typhoid fever before he could ever realize his dreams. The Fitkins established a memorial for their son. They gave 10,000 US dollars toward building a hospital in Swaziland.

At first, the plan was to build the hospital at the Endingeni Mission to the north. A Dr. West had come out to serve there. However, he could not be registered in the British protectorate, as his qualifications did not meet the British regulations. Eventually, he moved on to another mission field. However, during this time, God was preparing David Hynd to both fill the need for a hospital and to honor the Fitkins' son. In 1927 a fine Nazarene hospital was built and was named the Raleigh Fitkin Memorial Hospital.

Raleigh Fitkin Memorial Hospital. (This is a scanned painting by Marjorie Burne.)

There was nothing on the hilltop that had been chosen for the hospital but white ant (termite) hills and the stone and mud house built by the Hynd family. The place was full of anthills. Dr. David offered the Swazi children two shillings (twenty cents) for each ant queen dug out of a nest. Lots of children came to dig in the ant hills, and they found many queens. That helped minimize the proliferation of ants so that teams could begin to clear the ground and get it ready for building.

Building the hospital was a real challenge because the Swazis did not know how to build with bricks nor even with stone and mud. All their homes were beehive domes made of grass and thatch over a wooden frame. When clay was discovered in a swampy area in the valley behind the mission station, David Hynd learned to make and bake clay bricks. But before they went into making enough bricks to build a hospital, they had to go to the Chief and then to the King to get permission to use the clay to make the bricks.

Termites (white ants) in their red mud towers populated the hilltop like a city of skyscrapers and had to be moved to make way for the new hospital.

First, they made wooden molds in which to dry the clay into brick shapes. Next, they had to dig the clay out of the lagoon with picks and shovels. Then they packed the mud into the molds and left the clay bricks to dry in the sun. The bricks were repeatedly soaked with water on the outside as they dried slowly on the inside. Only when the bricks were totally dry—all the way through—were they stacked into a big square "furnace" tower where wood and kindling were burned to bake the clay bricks until they were dry and hard. Builders used these homemade bricks to build the Raleigh Fitkin Memorial Hospital.

The Fitkin family had provided the funds, the Chief and the King had given permission to use clay from the swampy lagoon, and Dr. David had learned how to prepare and fire the hard red bricks. All other building materials for the hospital had to be brought from Durban or Lourenzo Marques. It could take months to get material to the site. The hospital's builder was a local Swazi named Seth Hlophe, but Dr. David supervised much of the construction, even climbing up on the timbers to help with the gabled rafters.

One of the biggest obstacles of building, and indeed to the ability to treat patients effectively, was the fact that David did not speak any SiSwati. He could not even communicate with people in the local community. There was a man named Peter Dlamini who had worked at the gold mines in Johannesburg as a medical orderly. Each mine in Johannesburg had a sick bay area, and in each sick bay worked an African man who could help translate when people needed medical treatment. Peter had learned basic medical English and some rudimentary first aid.

Raleigh Fitkin Memorial Hospital was built of homemade clay bricks. There were two wards: one for females and one for males.

The Schmelzenbachs had learned about this man, and they asked him to come help Dr. David communicate with the Swazis who were having a hard time trusting this white man who wanted to treat their illnesses. While the hospital was being built, Peter and Dr. David went around the community on horseback giving medical aid and holding conferences.

*   *   *

One day, shortly before the hospital was completed, a boy was brought in because he had been run over by a *sledge*. Part of his leg had been torn away. His parents brought him to the Hynd's little hilltop home. The boy needed an operation. Just as the child arrived, Miss Robinson, a preacher lady from Endzingeni Mission, also arrived. Dr. David recruited all able-bodied people to help: Kanema, Miss Robinson, and Minah Maseko, a young girl helping in the kitchen at the time.

They put the lad on the kitchen table. Dr. David said to the visiting missionary lady, "Miss Robinson, you have to help me with this operation." Miss Robinson was assigned the task of holding the boy's leg while Dr. David performed an amputation. There was no one to give anesthesia, so Dr. David put chloroform in a bottle and said to his wife, "Put a cloth on the boy's nose and drop this chloroform on it so he will sleep." In that moment, Kanema became wife, mother, missionary, and anesthetist. They amputated the boy's leg. The child lived. It was amazing. This was Dr. David Hynd's first surgery in Swaziland.

After the surgery, they asked Minah to bring a bucket, and they dropped the leg in it. They then asked her to take it out. She picked up the bucket and went to do as she was told. However, as soon as she went out of the door, she fainted. Seeing a leg in a bucket was a new and frightening experience for her.

*   *   *

Soon the hospital was finished and patient care moved from the front veranda of the stone house to the new hospital. The finished hospital had a central area that was used as an outpatient department and an operating room for surgeries. It also had two wings—one for female patients and the other for male patients. It didn't matter what was wrong with you— whether it was typhoid, giving birth, or a foot problem, if you were female, you went to the female ward. If you were male, you went to the male ward. If it happened that there were not enough beds, the staff would place people on the floor where they lay on grass mats and covered by blankets.

Soon the first missionary nurse, Ms. Beleu, came from Scotland. Two other nurses came from the United States to join the staff. Another stone house was built on the hill so the single lady missionaries could have their own place to live. Raleigh Fitkin Memorial Hospital provided the first community health care ever available in Swaziland, and although the services were somewhat primitive, the staff gradually won the hearts and confidence of the Swazi people.

The second home built on a Manzini hilltop. It had a large dining and living area encircled by rooms that opened out to a verandah and into the communal area to provide for the increasing number of team members joining Dr. David and Kanema Hynd in serving the Swazi people.

Dr. David Hynd and Peter Dlamini continued going out and treating people in their homes. After a time, their work grew so big they couldn't go anymore. They asked the people to make their own carriers to bring patients to the hospital. Then the hospital began to be very busy.

There were other government hospitals in the country at the time: one in Hlathikhulu with one doctor, one in Mbabane that also had one doctor, and one at the Havelock asbestos mine in Bulembu to the north. With the increase in the number of hospitals, a new problem developed. There were no trained Swazi nurses to work in the hospitals. How could Dr. David find enough nurses to meet the need? The highest level of education necessary for these nurses, at the time, was standard three, which was only five years of school.

Original nursing students residential hall built in 1939.

Nothing was easy in Swaziland. First, Dr. David had to change Swazi custom because it stated that a person from one family could not look after a sick member of a different family due to the beliefs in familiar spirits that could jump from the patient to the helper. Slowly, Dr. David worked to change that custom because Christian principle says we must love and care for one another—no matter who that person is. The nurses, who were to be trained, needed a work of God's grace to enable them to care for *anyone* who came to the hospital.

Dr. David realized he had to train the nurses himself. This meant the student nurses did not have to leave the country to obtain training but could continue their education in Swaziland. He began with three students. Minah Maseko, the lady who fainted while carrying out the amputated leg, was one of the first of three Christian nurses to be enrolled in the school. She died recently at the age of ninety-three, having faithfully served for many years as the supervising nurse at the outstation clinic at Bhekinkhosi, about 30 km from the Manzini mission where she started her health care career by carrying out the severed leg in a bucket.

5

BACK HOME AGAIN

The Hynds arrived in Scotland for their first furlough in 1932. David spoke to many congregations about the great need for teachers in the country of Swaziland. Then he challenged the congregations to come and help. On one such occasion a teacher, Margaret Latta, responded and said she would come. She was not appointed or supported by a church but paid her own way from Uddingston, near Glasgow, to Swaziland, and sponsored herself by using insurance money she had received as compensation for a motor accident involving a bus.

By the time Ms. Latta came to Swaziland, the "school" classes Kanema had been teaching in her kitchen had already been moved from the house to the Stone Church. The first thing Ms. Latta did when she came to Swaziland was to build two more classrooms with stone walls and thatched roofs at the back of the Stone Church to accommodate the increasing number of students. (There were no windows in the buildings but only open spaces for light and air.) She moved the more advanced classes to these rooms, leaving the younger ones in the multipurpose space of the big Stone Church.

Together with Dr. David, she built the Nazarene Primary School in 1940, followed by the Nazarene High School in 1952, and finally, the Nazarene Teachers College in 1953. All of them were built of burnt red bricks made from clay from the swamp. Ms. Latta paid for all these buildings, using more of her funds from the compensation of the accident. There were no community schools at that time except for one government school at Matsapha—the Swazi National School started by King Sobhuza II. All other schools throughout the country had been

Nazarene Primary School, built in 1940, today has 700 lively young
students–the hope of the Nation.

The Nazarene High School, built in 1952, moved the academic level on the mission
station to secondary level–high school. Today it serves as the lower elementary grades
of the "Nazarene Practicing School." Student teachers use this school for their
practical training. Room 7 of this school was the very first teacher's training room
before the next building was completed.

started by church missions such as the Methodists, Catholics, Anglicans, Swedish, and Scandinavian missionaries.

David Hynd had great foresight as to what was needed, not only for the work he was doing but also for the whole country. He was a man of great vision. Samuel remembers that his father used to wake up as early as four o'clock in the morning to have his quiet time with the Lord. Then he would do a few tasks and some planning before going to the hospital to see patients.

David, together with Kanema, Ms. Latta, and a couple of Zimbabwean teachers had the vision of starting a teacher training college in Swaziland, so that instead of sending prospective teachers to Adams College in Natal, South Africa—the nearest college—for training, they could train at home. That's how a teacher training college began in Swaziland. First, they set up classes for prospective student teachers in the Stone Church. Miss Bertha Parker from Calgary, Canada, soon joined the teacher training team. The Nazarene Teachers Training College was the only one in the country until 1953 when the government set up another training centre at the Swazi National High School in Matsapha.

This is how the first nursing college and the first teacher training college in Swaziland ended up being located at the mission started by Dr. David. He is respected for all the work he did in Swaziland and for his huge vision of what was needed and what could be accomplished in the country.

*   *   *

David was a man of firsts. When the Hynds were in Scotland for their visit in 1932, they made contact with the Red Cross Society in London. They informed the Society that there was nothing like the Red Cross in Swaziland. So when they returned to Swaziland, they started a Red Cross chapter.

Similarly, David visited the London Bible Society and returned to start the Swaziland Bible Society. He formed a board and appointed a General Secretary, a Reverend Barnabus

Mndzebele who served for over 27 years. Dr. David also promoted the establishment of the Swaziland Conference of
Churches, bringing together the various Christian church
groups that had come into Swaziland for prayer, encouragement, and support. It was agreed, amongst themselves, that the
various missions groups would focus their efforts on reaching
the people in the four regions of the country. The Methodists
would focus on the south, where they had first brought the
Gospel into Swaziland in 1844. The Catholics would work in
the east, in the Lubombo Mountain Range adjacent to the Portuguese colony of Mozambique. The Church of the Nazarene
would concentrate its efforts in the northern and central areas.

Dr. David encouraged the formation of teachers' associations, as he also promoted the level of education in Swaziland.
He and Ms. Latta improved the level of education in all the
mission schools. The first level of graduation started at standard 3 (grade 5), then it was raised to standard 6 (grade 8),
then to standard 8 (grade 10), known as a Junior Certificate,
and up to matriculation in standard 10 (grade 12). As a result,
today the Church of the Nazarene has teachers, nurses, and
theological colleges that offer degree programs, all because of
the vision of David Hynd. The work he began continues. In
everything he did, he maintained a good working relationship
with the people of Swaziland. History has shown that the way
he did things was good for the people of the land.

Generally, little can be accomplished without conflict and
opposition, and Dr. David had his share of conflicts with other
missionaries who were already working in Swaziland. Most
missionaries emphasized doing one thing at a time, whereas
David emphasized balancing a number of projects that included literacy, education, and skills in training and development. He even established a working farm to supply milk,
emasi (Swazi yogurt), *mielies* (corn), beans, and other vegetables for the hospital and workers. He used the philosophy of
Jesus Christ's three-fold ministry: preaching, teaching, and
healing. Everything David did was based on the philosophy

of caring for and developing the whole person: body, soul, and spirit. It was a lesson his son, Samuel, learned well and has practiced throughout his life.

Some of the missionaries saw no need for teaching and nursing colleges in the country. These missionaries thought that one should only preach and not worry about the other requirements of life. But David refused to focus on only one aspect of the Swazi people's needs. He sought to meet as many of their needs as he could. He fought strong battles with many others, including government officials. Most missions groups focused solely on evangelism, but he understood that the converts could not grow spiritually if they could not read the Word of God or if they had no option but a traditional healer and the practice of witchcraft when they faced illness or accidents. Where would they go for help?

Nazarene Teacher Training College, the first in the country, built in 1953. It currently serves as the upper elementary school to the Nazarene Practicing School, as the Teacher Training College moved to new premises in the 1960s. Another 700 lively young students are learning here each day, preparing to serve the Nation as God-fearing citzens of tomorrow.

6

ONE STONE
AT A TIME

In the early days, Schmelzenbach had established a church under the trees at Mliba in the Lowveld area. A little later, he managed to build a stone and mud church building there. Dr. David would go there on Sundays and take the young Samuel with him. Slowly, the people came to know and to trust them and asked if there was any way David could help them. One day, the people said, "*siyafa,*" which means, "We are dying," and they were. They were dying from malaria, typhoid, and other tropical diseases.

In response to the pleading of the people, Dr. David began visiting some of the homes and helping these people. Malaria was the worst problem in the Bushveld. Hundreds of people died every summer when the mosquitoes were prevalent. Dr. David was able to help some, but the area was far from the main hospital—a distance of about sixty kilometres (thirty miles). People had to get a wagon or some other method of transport to bring their sick patients to the hospital. Some used a slip or a sledge and pulled it on the ground over the rough terrain using oxen or donkeys. Some were carried on the backs of relatives—often a mother or grandmother.

One day after a Sunday service, the people asked Dr. David if he could set up a clinic or *sibedlela*. David said that he had no funds or nurses to help at that time but that he would try to find a way. Since there was a road that came near the place, he first decided that once a month, he would come in his old Dodge open car with a canvas roof. When Samuel was on school holidays, he would accompany his father to Mliba and other similar outlying areas. The people flocked from miles around to see the *dokotela*.

Mliba Clinic – the first rural health centre was built with very thick walls using stones carried one at a time by worshippers when the community came to services and prayer meetings in the church. It still serves the community of Mliba, though it was expanded to provide more facilities and services.

It was not possible to build a brick clinic in that area because there was no clay or water source to make the bricks. There were, however, plenty of stones because the area was on a hill filled with stones. Dr. David told the people to bring a stone each time they came to church for services or prayers. He would use these to build a clinic. He and others loaded sand from a nearby river onto a sledge. The sledge was then pulled by oxen up to the church site, where the stones would be used for building the clinic—the first one in the country to serve the people of the Bushveld area. Finally, enough stones and sand were collected, and the clinic was built.

At that time, cement for construction projects was very difficult to obtain. As with all other building supplies, it had to be transported by ox-wagon from Durban in Natal, South Africa, or from Lourenzo Marques in Mozambique. To stretch the very scarce cement, the clinic builders used it only to point the stones and to set the corners of the clinic. The clinic still stands strong today and has very thick walls because the stones that were used were large.

A local white farmer at nearby Mbuluzi, a Mr. Wallace, saw the efforts being made to help the people. The Wallace family had come to Swaziland because after World War I ex-soldiers needed places to go to find work. Swaziland, as a British Protectorate, was divided into crown land, tribal land, and title deed land. Mr. Wallace was in the British armed forces during World War I and was entitled to farm land in Swaziland after the war. Now, he offered to provide timber for the rafters and the corrugated tiles for the clinic roof.

A couple of Indian builders had been recruited from Mozambique to build the RFM Hospital. Maugi, one of the Indian men, camped in the bush with a team of local people recruited to build this new stone and mud clinic. His team members all had to be supplied with malaria prophylactics (quinine) as the area was infested with malarial mosquitoes. Maugi stayed in Swaziland for the rest of his life. That stone clinic in the Bushveld still serves people today.

The Bushveld clinic was opened in 1931 without a resident nurse. Dr. David came once every four-to-six weeks to treat patients. At the same time he was making these trips, he was also developing the RFM Hospital staff. Dr. Mary Tanner from Glasgow, Scotland, completed her training and was sent out to help by the Church of the Nazarene World Missions Department. Not long after her arrival, she was on her way to a mission hospital exhibition in Johannesburg when she had an unfortunate car accident that left her scarred, and that limited her ability to serve in Swaziland. As soon as she was well enough to travel, she returned to Glasgow, Scotland, where she later married George Frame, a Scottish Nazarene pastor who was the superintendent of the British Isles Church of the Nazarene and a biographer of Dr. David Hynd.[1]

Note
1. Ibid.

7

PREPARATION FOR A LIFE OF SERVICE

When Samuel started his education it was at the same school for government servants' and expatriates' children in Bremersdorp that his sister, Isabel, attended. Due to their extensive commitments, Dr. David and Kanema were unable to take him to the school, so they had a young man—a worker at the mission—take him and Isabel on a donkey they had purchased. Samuel went to the Bremersdorp School for a term or two but then joined the multilevel classroom Swazi school, which, by this time, had moved from the kitchen floor veranda of his home to the Stone Church. Samuel was the only missionary child at the school. As a little child, he made good friends with the Swazi children and learned to speak SiSwati fluently. Many of the other children who attended were those of preachers or of teachers who were teaching at the school.

Samuel and sister, Isabel, going to school on a donkey.

Upon completing his primary school years, Samuel's parents were in a dilemma about where to send their son to school next. Their eldest child, Isabel, had gone to live in Scotland with her grandparents for her schooling. When her grandfather Sharpe had come for a mission supervisory visit, Isabel had returned to Scotland with him. However, Samuel was still too young for his parents to send him back to the United Kingdom on his own. Another missionary family had a similar situation. They too were from the British Isles and serving as missionaries with the International Holiness Mission that had recently amalgamated with the Church of the Nazarene at the Modderfontein Mission. They had two teenage sons, Reginald and Harold Jones. It was decided that the three boys should go together to St. Edwards boarding school in Johannesburg, as it was a bigger and better school than anything available at the time in Swaziland.

The year spent there was miserable for Samuel. He was amongst predominantly European (Caucasian) boys and no girls, and he was confined to the grounds of the boarding school. After years of being schooled with the Swazi children and having had the freedom of roaming the hills and mountains of Swaziland, city life and confinement was now unbearable. He had to find a way to convince his parents that St. Edwards was not the best situation for him.

It so happened that when Samuel was nine years old, a little girl was born to his parents. She was named Margaret Jane, and she grew up more like an only child since her elder sister and brother were away at school. She was a brilliant little girl but had few other children to play with, and her parents were ultra-busy with the development of the hospital, clinics, schools, colleges, and churches.

When she turned five years old, Samuel's parents decided that little Margaret should go to boarding school in Mbabane for her primary education. Samuel decided to use his little sister to his advantage. He convinced his parents that she would need the protection of her big brother in the school, as she was too young to be away from home. His parents agreed and transferred him back to St. Marks, the Anglican (Church of England) school in Mbabane, Swaziland, where they had registered Margaret.

Although he was still in boarding school, with the change of schools, he was in Swaziland and had the freedom to explore the mountains and rocks in the surrounding countryside around Mbabane. The boys swam and fished in rivers and challenged one another in all sorts of ways to climb the steep and high mountains. The oldest rocks in the world—carbon-dated back to the Pre-Cambrian era—are found in Pine Valley, just over the mountain ridge from Mbabane City. One of these rocks named Sibebe is the largest single rock in Africa and second only in the world to Ayers Rock in Australia. These great batholiths, which formed under the earth as volcanic rock, are some of the wonders of the world. The boys would explore and try to climb these great rocks.

The great rock was named for Sibebe. History tells us that Sibebe was a man who challenged one of the reigning kings in Swaziland. He was given the test of climbing this rock. If he succeeded, he would be given the Kingdom. Unfortunately for him, the rock is so steep that it is impossible to climb without ropes and chains. He fell to his death, and he did not take the Kingdom.

*　　*　　*

Samuel was thirteen when he gave his heart to the Lord and Savior, Jesus Christ of Nazareth. He was home for the school holidays and was attending a camp meeting service in Bremersdorp. One of the Swazi evangelists, Reverend Joseph Mkhwanazi, preached at the camp meeting. At the end of his message, he asked the young people if they wanted to invite this Jesus who stilled the oceans, healed the sick, and raised the dead, to come into their hearts, to rule and to reign in majesty and peace. Dr. Samuel says,

> Because of my knowledge of the language, it was as if Mkhwanazi was speaking directly to me. He was a "real" Swazi belonging to one of the original clans or families of Swaziland. What attracted me to him was that he was very active when he was preaching. I had heard lots of preachers, but this time something was

different. I didn't fall asleep when he was preaching. He held my attention. He acted out his sermons.

As he preached that day, I realized I needed Jesus. I wanted to be like the other Christians that I saw at the Mission Station. I responded to an old-fashioned altar call. I raised my hand, then went forward to the front of the crowd as a public witness of my choice to give my life to the risen Jesus as my Savior and Lord. I declared for all to know and see as the preacher said, "*Ngiyam ketsu Jesu*" which means, "I choose Jesus." That is what people in Swaziland did who wanted to be saved. I experienced a complete change.

My conversion set me on a new path. The school where I was enrolled in Mbabane, called St. Marks, was a Church of England boarding school. I took my newfound faith with me back to school where I started a prayer meeting under the gum trees. If we weren't playing sports, we would go to those trees and kneel

All Saints Anglican Cathedral church near St. Marks School
in Mbabane. It still serves the Nation today.

down there. We prayed that others would become interested and be converted. Anglicans prayed with a prayer book. Our group did not. We eventually built a little wooden enclosure that became our "church."

Because St. Marks was an Anglican or Church of England school, we were required to attend the All Saints Anglican Cathedral, a short distance from the school's boarding hostels, each week. This was rather high church and formal in style, so our little wooden "church" was a new step in the lives of many students, a little like the Upper Room in Jerusalem so long ago.

*   *   *

The meeting of Dr. Samuel and Joseph Mkhwanazi was an amazing paradox of God's grace. Samuel was a child in school. Joseph Mkhwanazi had been a herdsman from the south of Swaziland. He was a young man with wild, wooly hair. He was carrying a shield, a spear, an *assegai*,[1] and a *knobkerrie*[2] one day when he came across a small gathering of people under a thorny shade tree. A white lady was speaking to a group of people in their own language. He was fascinated and drew near to listen. This lady was a Norwegian missionary. Her name in SiSwati was "Mala Moe." She was a wonderful person based at Mlhosheni, a Scandinavian mission that had a church and a school in the southern part of the country. She shared how God had called her from her far away country to come to Africa and preach the good news of the saving grace of God.

Mkwanazi was astounded at the extent of God's love to send someone so far away to tell him about God's love. How did God even know he was in need of help? That day his life changed. He raised his hand saying he needed to know a God who had so much love that He came from Heaven as a human being and died on a hill outside of Jerusalem for Mkwanazi's sins. Then that same God sent someone from another world to come and tell him about this amazing love. He prayed, asking Jesus Christ to forgive him of every sin and every trespass.

He asked Jesus to come into his life and to rule and reign as sovereign Lord and King. He put aside his *lihawu* (cow skin shield) and took up the shield of faith. He put aside the *assegai* (spear) and took up the sword of the Word of God. He went to live on the Mission Station, learned to read and write, studied the Bible with the missionaries, and became an ordained evangelist. So it was that God saved and prepared this man of God, Joseph Mkhwanazi, to bring a young son of a missionary, Samuel Hynd, living far from the land of his birth, to be born again of the Spirit of God.

Young Samuel was a new man from that day onward. He no longer travelled on trips to clinics and wayside gatherings under the trees at preaching points *just* to be with his father. Now he went as his father's partner. On one occasion, they were at a clinic where lines and lines of people waited to be helped. Samuel, because he was on school holiday, was there with his father. Samuel remembers that sick people crowded around them. There were so many people that his father could not possibly take care of all of them before the sun set and the people had to return home. It looked as if they wouldn't be able to finish before nightfall, so Dr. David separated all the people needing tooth extractions from those with other medical needs. There were no dentists in the country. Rotten teeth had to be removed to prevent pain and further infections in the body.

"One old woman had a bad tooth that needed to be removed," Dr. Samuel said. "Even though I was a young teenager, my dad handed me the necessary tool and told me to take it out for her. He said to clamp the tool on the tooth, wiggle it a little, then pull, and it would come out cleanly. I was stunned. *Me, take out a tooth?* But since there was no other option and the woman in pain, I was willing. I put the tool in her mouth, clamped the tooth, wiggled it a little, and pulled. The tooth came out, and the woman was all smiles."

Samuel became a medical assistant, and it was then he realized that deep in his heart he too had a passion to train and become a medical missionary doctor and ordained minister like his father. He too wanted to help the Swazi people. This set the path for his life. From the age of thirteen onward, he has never wavered or hesitated in his commitment to the Lord Jesus Christ, nor in his commitment to serve the people of Swaziland.

*   *   *

Toward the end of World War II when Samuel was completing high school at St. Marks Secondary School in Mbabane, he was nominated Head Boy of the school by the faculty. This meant he was found to be responsible, honest, faithful, and diligent in school and in social relationships. As Head Boy he was responsible for all of the other students' behavior and for seeing to it that they accomplished their duties. He worked with a team of three or four other senior high school boys who were nominated as prefects.

In those days, all the high school students lived in the boarding hostel. The boys' dorm was Duncan House, and the girls' dorm was Alice Vine House. There was only cold water in the dormitories, so the boys showered in cold water. Single male schoolteachers, who also lived in the dormitories, supervised them. "As Head Boy, I had a room to myself away from the dormitory and next to the school master," Samuel remembers. "We ate all our meals in the school dining hall."

Students had to study very hard to complete the high school examinations called the "Joint Matriculation Board." One of Samuel's subjects was Latin because he wanted to read medicine. "There was no teacher to teach Latin at the school, so my father, who served on the school board, arranged for me to go to the home of the National Director of Education, Mr. Glynn, appointed from London, to learn Latin which would prepare me for the study of medicine," Dr. Samuel remembers. "Mr. Glynn was the only person in Swaziland who could read and write Latin."

*   *   *

Samuel Hynd became a young man of purpose, direction, inspiration, and determination. When he finished his primary and high school education, he entered the University of Witwatersrand in South Africa. Some of his student friends later became world-renowned. One such friend was Dr. Phillip Tobias, whose work in anthropologic research of early man set him apart in that field. The two studied medicine together at university. They stood, side by side, cutting up cadavers and experimenting in the chemistry and physics labs.

During his training, Samuel lived in Johannesburg and rarely had the opportunity to visit his family in Swaziland, even though Swaziland is not all that far away. In the 1940s, World War II came. Samuel was not called into full-time military service as he was in medical school. However, he enlisted in the South African army, first in the artillery division. Later he was transferred to the medical corp. He never went on active duty, but it was only because of timing. His corp was called up, and they embarked on their journey to Durban where they were to board a ship for Madagascar. The Vichy French had joined the Germans and were at war with the Allies. South Africans were called to go and deal with a remnant of these Vichy French in the Indian Ocean. Just as they were about to set sail from Durban harbour, the Vichy French surrendered, and the men were turned back and sent home or back to their schools to continue their education. Dr. Samuel never once fired a shot. He was spared the trauma of a war-torn world.

While he was in university, he lived with friends of his parents, the Robertsons. They lived in Auckland Park, a suburb of Johannesburg. Samuel would ride a bicycle to the University each day. Since there were no Nazarene Churches in the city at that time, Samuel chose Central Baptist Church as his place to worship.

Shortly before the war, Isabel came back to Africa. She returned to do nurses' training at Johannesburg General Hospital. Later she studied midwifery in Boksburg-Benoni Hospital. Because of the war, no one could travel, not even for further study; so Isabel returned to Swaziland and worked in Raleigh

Fitkin Memorial Hospital with her parents for three years. Little sister, Margaret, was still in school in Mbabane.

Isabel and Margaret Hynd, Dr. Samuel's older and younger sisters.

In 1946, once World War II was over and people could safely travel once more, the Hynd family took its second furlough and returned to Scotland and the British Isles to visit family and churches. Samuel had, by now, completed his Bachelor Degree in Medical Science from the University of Witwatersrand, South Africa. He travelled with his family to the UK to enroll for further training. His sisters, Isabel and Margaret, also returned to Scotland with the family.

"I went with my parents, and was accepted as a medical student at the University of Glasgow. I stayed with my grandfather, Rev. Dr. George Sharpe, in the manse (parsonage) while going to university. It took about three years for me to complete my schooling and become a doctor. I knew, by then, I wanted to practice medicine in Swaziland. During school holidays, I was attached to clinics where I could practice medicine. You went to the classroom to learn about a disease, and then you went to the ward to see a patient who fit those symptoms," he said.

University of Glasgow where Dr. Samuel graduated, M.B., Ch.B. Degree in Medicine in 1949.

Not only did he stay with his grandfather, but he also became involved in the church his grandfather had established at Parkhead. He led the young people as president of the Nazarene Youth International (NYI). He was active in recruiting and involving the young people of the Parkhead Church in many activities, including the rescue of nearby Kilmanock Church, which was dying. He did this by mobilizing young people to come into the situation and bring life and focus to this church. It would have died without their assistance.

His best friend, during these years, was Samuel Doktorian, a young Armenian man whose family had escaped to the UK from the genocide of his people in the Middle East. The two Samuels, Samuel Doktorian and Samuel Hynd, led Bible meetings at the university, in the communities of Glasgow, and in the steel factory area where the church was located. The steel factory area was plagued with drunks and disillusioned work-

Opening of the new Parkhead Church of the Nazarene, 33 Burgher Street, Glasgow. Dr. Samuel Hynd prayed the dedication and cut the ribbon September 2013.

ers from all over Scotland who had come to the city hoping to make good in Glasgow's steel industry. Many failed and sought comfort in alcohol. These two young, university students held street rallies, youth camps, and youth services, bringing the Gospel to the young people of Glasgow, Scotland, and other nearby churches. Later, Doktorian became a world-renowned preacher, teacher, and prophet in the Christian world. He established the Bible Lands Bible College in Lebanon.

Graduation Ceremony on 9 July, 1949,
at the University of Glasgow, Scotland.
Dr. Samuel Hynd celebrating with great
joy and pride with his sister and lifelong
friend, Isabel Hynd.

Samuel excelled in his studies and in his Christian walk. He was ordained as a minister of the Gospel by the Church of the Nazarene. After a time, his parents and Margaret returned to Swaziland to continue the work there. Samuel and Isabel stayed behind in Scotland, and he completed his studies. Isabel became the nursing supervisor and director of a children's home in East Glasgow, near where the family had lived.

A little later on, Dr. Samuel's sister, Margaret, decided to follow the family way of medical missions service. She went to Epworth College in Pietermaritzburg in Natal, a province of South Africa, where she excelled at her studies. She was valedictorian, and her name is still on the Honor Roll Board at the entrance of the school.

Having seen how hard her father and brother worked, she decided to study physiotherapy instead of medicine at the University of Witwatersrand where Samuel had attended. There she was very active in student Christian events and lived at the YWCA (Young Women's Christian Association) in Braamfontein, within walking distance of the University. Upon graduation, she too felt the call to missions and applied where she was most at home—with the Department of World Missions of the Church of the Nazarene in Kansas City, Missouri. She interviewed as a missionary but was declined as the General Board of the Department of World Missions said they had no need to send physiotherapists to the mission field. Today, however, the RFM Hospital has a physical therapy department, intensive care unit (ICU), and even a dental clinic.

Margaret then went to Glasgow, Scotland, and lived with her Uncle Victor and Aunt Isabel Edwards (her mother's younger sister) to study medicine at Glasgow University School of Medicine, as her father and brother had done before her. She excelled in academics and completed her degree in medicine. She reapplied to the Department of World Missions and was joyfully accepted, and was sent to Acornhoek Hospital with Dr. Harold Jones

The Graduate, Dr. Samuel Hynd, with his degree in Medicine and Surgery (M.B., Ch.B.), a milestone accomplished as he looked forward to future decades with confidence and great anticipation.

and Dr. and Mrs. Paul Merki to serve in what had been an International Holiness Mission among the Swazi people. It was located across the South African border near Kruger National Park. This mission had a Bible College, a primary and secondary school, and a church at Arthurseat, about five miles away from the Acornhoek Medical Hospital in what was the Eastern Transvaal at that time—now it is Mphumalanga, in the eastern province of South Africa. She served as a diligent and careful doctor and was well loved and trusted by her patients.

While assisting another attending surgeon, she had an unfortunate accident. The surgeon's hand slipped and sliced Margaret's hand through her gloves. She contracted hepatitis, and that debilitated her and compromised her health for the rest of her life. She could not recover in the heat of Africa, which aggravates any liver condition. She returned to the UK and lived with her sister Isabel in London until she had recovered her health. She did well in England's cooler climate and was able to return to her studies, specializing in anesthesiology.

She then returned to medical missions in Africa but not with the Church of the Nazarene, as all their medical facilities were located in the middle and lowveld areas that were too hot for her to manage her health. She first returned to Mbabane and worked in private practice with Dr. Stephenson to see if her health would hold up, then she plunged back into Mission Hospitals working high on the Ubombo Mountain ranges at Bethesda Mission, then to Themba Hospital in the hills near Nelspruit, South Africa, where she was promoted to medical superintendent of the hospital. After successfully managing the hospital for some years, the South African government took over all the mission hospitals, and Dr. Margaret became a civil servant. Just at this time, her parents moved to the capital city of Mbabane from the Leper Colony in Swaziland and needed more help, so she moved back to Swaziland and rented a house next door to her aging parents. This was a blessing to them as Margaret stayed close by until Kanema Hynd passed away and Dr. David moved to Manzini and lived in a cottage next to his son Samuel on the Elwandle range overlooking Manzini and the Nazarene Mission station that he founded. Margaret then moved back to South Africa and was appointed Medical Superintendent of the Barbeton Hospital in Mphumalanga. She continued serving the Swazi people across the border.

After Samuel graduated from medical school, he followed in his father's footsteps to the London Royal College of Tropical Medicine and Hygiene. He moved to London immediately upon graduation from medical school. At this point, he had not yet learned to treat tropical diseases, as most of the illnesses presented by the patients in Scotland were pneumonia and other city diseases found in the northern hemisphere. Samuel knew he was going to spend his life serving the Swazi people who lived in the southern hemisphere and who, therefore, suffered from malaria, typhoid, leprosy, tuberculosis, and bilharzia.

At that time, nearly every child in Manzini had bilharzia. It was imperative that he study under highly qualified people from around the world who had come to teach on diseases found in Africa, Asia, India, and the Americas. It would take him about a year to get a degree from this graduate college.

"When I first came to Swaziland, people would line up to be treated for bilharzia and amoebic dysentery. It's so much better now. Today, children are educated about how to avoid contracting these diseases," he says.

In London, Samuel rented a room in Kensington, near where his sister, Isabel, lived. She had also moved to London and had gone to work at Glaxo Pharmaceutical Company as an industrial nurse. She spent the rest of her working years with this company caring for the researchers, scientists, lab technicians, and workers in many laboratories and research centres throughout the London area.

There were no Nazarene churches in London at that time. Arthur Noble, a Scottish friend, knew a family that attended a Baptist church. This family invited Samuel to church for an evening service, and after the services, they hosted what was called a "squash" meeting. "Squash" was the buzzword for a young people's gathering after church for discussion, prayer, coffee, and doughnuts. It was called "squash" as all the participants were squashed into the small living rooms of their student flats or their friends' homes.

"While I was there sitting on a stool," Dr. Samuel said, "this young woman walked in, and I literally fell off the chair. It was love at first sight. I went to the wife of my host and asked her to introduce me. The young woman's name was Rosemarie Sylvia Ballard."

Samuel's first invitation to her for a date was to a play called *The Gates of Hell*. It was a musical of splendid truth and vivid drama about the consequences of our choices in life—a choice to accept a relationship with God our Creator or a choice to reject the Creator and find ourselves on the path to death and destruction. "I don't suppose it was the best place to take the one you are trying to win," Dr. Samuel chuckles as he remembers now.

After the play, the two walked to Trafalgar Square for a cup of tea and then to Hammersmith to catch the underground train to Ealing, where Rosemarie's home was located. After delivering her home, Samuel then caught the bus back to Kensington to his one-room flat, which was close to the medical college.

Rosemarie was young. She had just finished high school at Haberdashers College in London and had begun working. Her family was Anglican (Church of England). She, however, had left her traditional church after she was born again in a Baptist gathering where her friends attended. She was eager to know the life of Christ and to serve the Lord with all her heart.

"While I was getting to know Rosemarie, I discovered she had a call to be a missionary. I invited her to get to know the Nazarenes. We went to the district assembly for the British Isles Church of the Nazarene, which was being held in Glasgow, Scotland. I introduced her to Dr. Samuel Young, the general superintendent of the Nazarene churches presiding in Scotland, for an interview as a missionary candidate."

Samuel Young had been born and raised in Scotland, but his family had moved to the United States. Before becoming general superintendent, he had been the president of Eastern Nazarene College in Quincy, Massachusetts, USA. Dr. Young suggested Rosemarie needed to become acquainted with the Church of the Nazarene. He thought it would be wise for her to go to Eastern Nazarene College so that she would understand the Nazarenes and their ways. Dr. Young found a scholarship for her to go to Boston. She went and was greatly blessed by the Nazarene people and her studies there. This was amazing since Rosemarie's parents were Anglican, but it was not a strange choice as her father's sister, her aunt, and her aunt's husband were Salvation Army missionaries in India.

Samuel's eyes still shine as he continues his story. "We were so excited after her interview that we bought fish and chips on Toll Cross Road. The food was wrapped in newspaper, as that was the way fish was served in those times. We walked six miles back to London Road where we were staying with my Aunt Isabel, who was now married to Victor Edwards, a Church of Scotland pastor."

London Road House, Glasgow, Scotland. This was Samuel Hynds' home during his university years in Glasgow. His bedroom window is above the front door.

After Samuel and Rosemarie had dated for only a short time, Samuel approached Rosemarie's parents to ask for her hand in marriage. It was then he gave them the shocking news that he was destined to become a medical missionary in Swaziland, Africa, and if they agreed to let him marry their daughter, she would go with him to Africa. They wanted to know where she would live. Dr. Samuel couldn't resist. "I think the devil got in me," he laughs. "I told them that Rosemarie's and my home would be a grass thatch hut (a *kraal*) with an opening for the door that was about half a man's height so that if a wild animal or intruder came in, they could hit the intruder on the head before any damage could be done to them inside the hut. Her parents were shocked. Then I relented and told them she

Grandpa, Dr. David Hynd, crawling out the doorway of a Swazi grass thatch home.

would be living in a proper house. It's amazing that her parents agreed to let her marry me."

To prepare herself for life on the mission field, Rosemarie went to Quincy, Massachusetts, and studied so that she could be of assistance in the Raleigh Fitkin Memorial Hospital. While she was in college in Quincy, Samuel proceeded to Swaziland, where he worked with his father. By now the hospital had grown and had 350 beds with a maternity department, an outpatient department, an emergency room, a theatre for surgeries, and an X-ray department with a donated machine. This X-ray machine used so much electricity that Samuel's mother, Kanema, had to phone everyone in town to turn off all of their electrical appliances and lights during the lunch hour so she could take any needed x-rays.

In Swaziland, Samuel worked in both the main RFM Hospital and the rural community clinics that David had established. At the time, there were only two other doctors at the hospital: Dr. David Hynd and Dr. Seamand. The three doctors had to rotate. Each of them tried to take at least one weekend off per month. They worked night and day as people now knew the clinics and hospital were places to come for help in times of trouble. They routinely dealt with typhoid, malaria, serious burns, cattle herding injuries—like the disemboweling of a man by a bull—and all kinds of hard-to-imagine illnesses and injuries.

Some of the most common injuries were head injuries. "When I first began to practice in Swaziland, many surgeries

Dr. Samuel arriving in Africa to serve with his parents Dr. David and Rev. Kanema Hynd.

were compression fractures because of fights the men had with the *knobkerrie*," Dr. Samuel remembers. "Dr. David was an expert in this kind of surgical repair. One day he asked me to deal with such an injury. I used a chisel for that first case. I tried to lift the compressed skull bones off the brain. After trying for an hour, I was still battling with this skull. I was afraid the chisel would go right through the patient's head. Dr. David found me tap, tap, tapping, and he said, 'Are you still doing this? Let me help you.' He put on an extra pair of surgical gloves and took an instrument and a chisel and said, 'Just watch me.' My father had done many procedures of this kind. He went whack, whack!" Dr. Samuel laughs. "In seconds the skull bones came up to relieve the pressure on the patient's brain. I felt like a fool, but I soon became an expert at fixing this problem myself, as it was quite common."

The three main clinics were in Siteki, Endingeni, and Piggs Peak. They had to be visited monthly as there were no doctors at those clinics. They were run by missionary nurses. The clinic at Mliba was the one built of mud and stone. It had been established, but it did not have even one missionary nurse. The clinic was operated by one of the Swazi graduates from Dr. David's school of nursing, Martha Dlamini.

Missionary and Swazi Medical family in 1950 when Dr. Samuel joined the team.

Crossing the Great Usutu River on the way to Piggs Peak on the hand-powered "Pont," as no bridges had been built but patients needed to be reached and nurses needed a doctor's visit once per month.

*   *   *

Samuel continued his work in Africa and wrote letters to Rose-marie in the USA. It took weeks and sometimes months for their letters to crisscross the land and sea between New England and Swaziland. They continued their romance until she had completed her studies in the USA and was ready to marry. Then it was time for Samuel to return to the United Kingdom where he would meet and collect his bride.

Samuel travelled four days by plane from Africa to England: It was one day from Johannesburg to Nairobi, where the passengers spent the night. Then he went on to Khartoum in Sudan, then to Cairo, Egypt, where the passengers spent another night, then Malta, and finally into Bournemouth Airport in the South of England.

It's interesting the scenes that get seared into our minds. Dr. Samuel remembers such a scene. "Just before we landed, I looked down and there was a lady with a pram and a young child," Dr. Samuel said. "I looked down and the child looked up. I've never forgotten that little face gazing out of a fluffy hat." His Aunt Isabel came to meet him at the airport, and they went from there to London by train and north to Nantwich, England.

Rosemarie had crossed the Atlantic Ocean from New England to meet Samuel in Nantwich for their wedding. (In 1950 her parents had moved away from Ealing near London to Nantwich, near the city of Crewe, in the midlands of England. She chose to be married in Nantwich.) She did not have many friends in that area, but all of Samuel's Scottish friends and relatives came from Scotland for the wedding. They brightened up the party with their fun and frolics.

The wedding was held in a beautiful Church of England Abbey (rented for the occasion) with a pipe organ and choir. Then, much to the shock and surprise of the English, a Scotsman, Robert Yeats, started playing the bagpipes to accompany the bride down the aisle. Some of the English people in the crowd actually thought a catfight had erupted in the belfry, as they had never heard Scottish bagpipes warming up. Once the

Wedding: Samuel and Rosemarie full of life and joy, expectation and excitement
of life together in Africa (September 1951).

piper filled the bag of his instrument with air, the ethereal
sound of the highlands of Scotland filled the abbey, and the
bride walked down the aisle on the arm of her father, Stanley
George Ballard, in splendor.

Robert Yeats and bagpipes outside Church of England Abbey in Nantwich, England.

The reception was held on the village green. After the reception, friends of the bridegroom came to help the bride and groom get ready for their happy send off to Africa and their new life together. Samuel and Rosemarie changed into travel clothes. As they emerged, beautifully dressed, they were lifted onto the shoulders of their friends and carried bodily across the village green (a very Scottish tradition) to the train station where their bags were loaded onto the baggage car. There, their friends bid them farewell. Some friends joined them on the train, and much to the amusement of all, the confetti in their train compartment was knee deep. It blew out of the open windows and fell on passersby as the train sped through the countryside.

What neither Samuel nor Rosemarie knew, but were about to find out, was that their suitcases were also filled with confetti. When they were aboard the Union Castle ocean liner called The Windsor Castle, they opened their bags and steamer trunks to a shower of confetti falling like snow and covering everything in their cabin. It was a dead giveaway to the other passengers that they were newlyweds.

Boarding the Windsor Castle at South Hampton, England. Rosemarie is beneath the gang-plank ready to board and begin a new life in a new land with new people.

When they arrived in Cape Town, a car—a gift from Ms. Robinson, a USA missionary—awaited them. Dr. Samuel and his bride took a honeymoon trip before returning to Swaziland.

The car driven to Cape Town by Dr. Samuel's father for the newlyweds' adventure into Africa.

The trip took several days and gave Samuel a chance to introduce his London bride to life in Africa. For the first time, she saw elephants in the Knysna forests in the east coast of Africa. In Durban, South Africa, Rosemarie swam in the waves of the Indian Ocean, which were bigger than any she had seen in America or England. The two played like children, jumping over breakers, as the waves came rolling onto the sandy beaches.

In time, they arrived in Bremersdorp. There is no way Rosemarie could have prepared for what she encountered there. As they drew near the hospital, someone put his hand through the car window and shut off the engine. Then those outside the car physically pushed it to the hospital where everyone was waiting. Swazi people and missionaries were gathered in front of the hospital to greet the newlyweds with singing, jumping up and down with joy, making speeches, and giving gifts.

The young couple first lived with Samuel's parents in a two-story house called, "The Big House," which his mother had built with funds from an inheritance her father had given her. Many missionaries and pastors from all over Southern Africa came to RFM hospital for help. If they came to be with a hospitalized family member, they were always welcome to stay at the Big House. Patients who were no longer sick enough to stay in the hospital, but not well enough to go back to their outstation homes, stayed there as well. Kanema Hynd willingly provided hospitality for these friends and families as a gift to Christ Jesus.

God was good to Samuel and Rosemarie and provided funds through a church in the USA for them to build a family home at the mission station. The couple designed the home of their dreams, and Rosemarie never did have to live in a grass hut and beat off wild animals.

The mission gate through which the young couple was welcomed and then led to the front steps of RFM Hospital.

The couple planned to have four children, and they hoped to spend the rest of their lives in the service of God in Bremers-dorp (Manzini.) Some of the many things Rosemarie had to learn besides the SiSwati language were the customs of the

Swazi culture. In those days, married Swazi women wore their hair in what was called "a beehive of hair" and covered it with a brightly-coloured scarf. Obviously, Caucasian hair could not be manipulated into the beehive style, so in compromise, the white women were asked to wear a hat.

"Big House" built with Kanema Hynd's inheritance from her father, Rev. Dr. George Sharpe, that served as the young couple's first home shared with the elder Hynds.

Swazi married women also wore a long, heavy, skin skirt, usually made of goatskins. The furry side of the skin would be on the outside and would be decorated. The smooth side would be on the inside against their bare legs. The skin had to be softened by applying loads of animal fat and oil. They ladled this fat from the top of the stew when they boiled meat. The skins were very heavy and were never washed. Western women were not required to wear the skin skirts, but they were asked to wear their skirts below the knee to be seen as decent among the community.

Life was golden, and the sunny skies over peaceful Swaziland promised a life of challenge, meaning, and purpose for these young newlyweds. However, Swazi life could also be challenging. One day a small snake made its way into the Big House. Rosemarie was startled to find such a beautiful, green, slithery creature in the house. She ran to her mother-in-law asking what was to be done. Kanema said, "That snake is more afraid of you than you are of it. Just take the hockey stick from the coat rack, pick it up, and throw it out the door." Rosemarie was not sure that plan would be successful, so she took the hockey stick and tried to beat the snake to death. It wriggled out of the way of all her attempted murderous strikes. Finally, the poor creature escaped out the open door and fled for cover in the bushes. It was true that the snake was more afraid of Rosemarie than she was of it. It just wanted to find a way to freedom. That was the last time she tried to kill a snake.

Notes

1. A long pole spear used commonly in Southern Africa as a weapon.
2. The knobkerrie is a handheld weapon made from the hard knot of a tree and used to kill snakes as folks walk through the bush. On occasion it was used to thump someone over the head causing a deadly fracture and/or brain damage. Both definitions are from www.wikepedia.com, sourced on April 28, 2014.

8

IN THE SERVICE OF KINGS

Immediately after Samuel's arrival in Swaziland in 1950, Dr. David took him to meet King Sobhuza II. Dr. David, Dr. Samuel, and His Majesty met in the King's office. It was the place where King Sobhuza later built the magnificent Lozitha Palace and where He and His successor, King Mswati III, even today meet international visitors.

"I'll never forget the day when my father introduced me to King Sobhuza II," Dr. Samuel said. "I had seen the King on

His Majesty King Sobhuza II who embraced Samuel Hynd as a *"Dlamini"* drawn into the Royal family "BantfabeNkhosi."

occasion at special events, but I had never met Him before. Now that I was medically qualified, my father felt this was the right time to be officially introduced to the King.

"It was a Sunday afternoon when Father brought me to meet the King. He was wearing the traditional dress of a skin skirt, beads, and feathers in his hair. I was wearing a suit. The King was delighted that I had returned 'home' to share in my father's work. Then the King shared His heart concerning the challenges of His Nation. My father told Him that I was going to be the one caring for the Royal family. This included being their doctor and being His ambassador to all the missionaries and pastors from other countries."

Dr. David had been the Royal family's personal physician. Depending on what level of royalty the patient was, either a car came to collect Dr. David, or the Royal person would be brought to RFM Hospital. In the case of His Majesty, the King, Dr. David went to wherever His Majesty was. The King rarely travelled, but once went to London with a group of elders and advisors to settle land issues between the British, the Afrikaners, and the Portuguese. This was in the days when Swaziland was still a British Protectorate with Queen Victoria as the Head of State and King Sobhuza II as what was called "Paramount Chief," although in the eyes of the Swazis, He was still the King of Swaziland. Dr. David went along on this trip.

On the day Dr. Samuel met the King, the session ended with the three men on their knees praying. The King loved to pray, and He exemplified all of the Christian values in his life. As a child, the King had been sent to school at a Methodist Mission in the Transkei, across the Kei River, to be educated — the same school as the son of the Xhosa chief, Nelson Mandela, who later became the first black president of South Africa. "I realized at my first meeting with King Sobhuza II that I had been called home to Swaziland for a reason," said Dr. Samuel. The meeting set the tone for the rest of Dr. Samuel's life, as he began to minister to the whole man: body, soul, and spirit.

*   *   *

Dr. David and the King had a very good relationship despite their differences in culture and beliefs. The King was a gracious man. He was a man of peace, wisdom, and integrity. He knew the Bible well, and some of His messages were so powerful it was as if they were from a renowned preacher.

As the years wore on, King Sobhuza II and Dr. Samuel also became good friends and they were as close as the King and Dr. David had been. "My kids remind me of when He would come to the house in the middle of the night with all His escorts and sit in our lounge to discuss matters with me and his elders. This was always exciting for the kids—dogs barking, car lights shining, police and soldiers in traditional dress searching the house and premises."

King Sobhuza reached out to Dr. Samuel for wisdom as they talked together during those night visits. One day the King said to Dr. Samuel, "You are a *Dlamini*." *Dlamini* is the name of the Royal family. Calling Dr. Samuel a *"Dlamini"* was an honor of the highest kind because He was calling him family. The King had confidence in Dr. Hynd's character, wisdom, and friendship. There probably was no one else in His life with whom He could have had that kind of relationship.

In 1973, King Sobhuza became ill with leukemia. "The King gave me a free hand to do what I needed to do for him. He sent me to London to find a specialist in leukemia, and for ten years we extended his life through blood transfusions." Dr. Samuel had to get all the tribal chiefs' permission to do transfusions because it meant taking another person's blood and putting it into the King. "I had to sit with all the chiefs in a big hall and explain to them at length what it meant to take blood from a donor and transfuse it into the King. These chiefs had much power. I had to explain how it would work in His body. Then I had to tell them, 'Take your choice; do you want Him to live or die? The blood transfusions will give Him life.' They finally agreed we could transfuse Him."

Some years before the onset of the King's illness, Dr. David and Dr. Samuel had established an ICU unit at a place called "Mr. John's Dairy Farm" near the town of Malkerns, not far from Matsapha where the airport was located. When The King became desperately ill with leukemia, he went to the farm for treatment. Sharon Jones, a Nazarene missionary from Indiana, USA, was a trained ICU nurse. "She became the King's intensive care nurse, and did an excellent job of nursing Him. "We treated Him without administering drugs and used only blood transfusions," said Dr. Samuel. This was long before his symptoms became serious. At that time, we did not have the modern medications to treat leukemia as we do now." The King knew Dr. Samuel was doing everything in his power to help extend His life and make it as bearable as possible.

In spite of his illness, the King had great wisdom. One day when the King was sick, Dr. Samuel went to check on Him. A man came in while he was there and talked to the King about a lot of things another man had done. After he finished talking, the King said to him, "Tomorrow at this time, the man you are talking about will be here. You must come and repeat yourself." The first man did not come back the following day, revealing that what he had told the King was not true, and the King, with His wisdom, had exposed his falsehood.

After many years of careful treatment, the King's condition finally worsened. "I was in an American-styled camp meeting when a car arrived. A man got out and said, 'You are wanted, please come quickly!' I hurried to the King's bedside. I reached out to touch Him and found He was having difficulty breathing. Moments later, He died in my hands," Dr. Samuel remembers.

"The present governor of Ludzidzini (the Royal Residence), T. V. Metwa, was with me in the room when the King breathed His last. One of the princes was also there. It was a shock to the Nation that He had passed away, so His body was kept in Malkerns for a time to give the Nation time to absorb the tragedy. He was then prepared for burial, and the Nation mourned His loss. In a few days, the funeral was held at Lobamba, near the main road. The King's body was then taken to the sacred Royal, burial grounds in the south of Swaziland."

*   *   *

A number of years earlier in 1968, Dr. Samuel had been attending to the hundreds of outpatients who came daily to the RFM Hospital, when he was summoned to come quickly to the Queens' Maternity Ward because LaTwala was giving birth. Dr. Samuel jumped up from the consulting desk and ran through the corridors of the hospital down to the maternity ward and found Ellen Magongo, the attending midwife, flustered yet relieved that he had come. Within a few minutes, a beautiful baby boy popped out of his mother and into the hands of Dr. Samuel who lifted him high by his feet and smacked his bottom so that he would take in his first breath. Dr. Samuel recalls, "I heard the most marvelous speech of his life as he let out a strong, bold cry and breathed life into his lungs. Never have I heard any speech sweeter or more majestic in all my days."

It was this young wife and mother, LaTwala who had been attending to the King at the farm turned ICU centre in Malkerns. Unbeknownst to her, her role would soon change. The elders convened to decide who was to be appointed the next King of the Swazis. Politics becomes serious at these times. Deliberations proceeded as the elders sought to identify the next king. The Queen Mother, Dzeliwe, one of the older wives of King Sobhuza II, had been serving as the *Indlovukazi*.[1] She was now identified as Head of State and Queen Regent. The children of King Sobhuza II had all gathered from various parts of the world to participate in their

His Majesty King Mswati III.

father's burial. One of the young princes, Makhosetive, had been in school in England and had also returned for the funeral of his father. This young man was born the year Queen Elizabeth II granted our Nation independence.

The elders selected this baby, now a young teenager, Prince Makhosetive, to be the Crown Prince of Eswatini— the Kingdom of Swaziland. "I did not know that day in 1968, that I was holding the future King of Swaziland, Mswati III, in my hands and

LaTwala did not know she was to become the next *Indlovukazi* of Swaziland," Dr. Samuel said. After the funeral of His father, the young Crown Prince went back to school in the UK for two or three years before He was fully crowned King Mswati III and took office.

"After the death of Sobhuza II, I was no longer the Royal family's physician until King Mswati III started travelling. Then I was called back to the position of personal physician and traveled with the King."

Dr. Samuel travelled with His Majesty to Malaysia where the King attended the Commonwealth Heads of State meeting. The King requested that Dr. Samuel call his daughter, Elizabeth, to come immediately from Hong Kong to Kuala Lumpur. She came and joined in the meetings. Each morning, Dr. Samuel led devotions with His Majesty. During one of devotional times, the King spoke to Elizabeth and asked why she was giving her talents to Asia instead of Swaziland when Swaziland needed her talents so much.

Traveling with His Majesty on a state visit to Taiwan, Republic of China.

For Elizabeth it was part of a process that had begun earlier, and the King's question confirmed God's call for her to return to Swaziland where she was born. Later on, she opened a home for orphans of the AIDS pandemic. She tells her story in a book called *A Little Child Shall Lead Them*.[2]

"I travelled many other places with King Mswati III. Once we went to Cypress via Switzerland. A few years later, we went first to New York, USA, where the King gave a speech at the United Nations, and then we went on to Washington, DC, to meet with the US President. There were many trips to Taiwan, Brunei, Japan, Europe, and to various African states.

"I remember that once His Majesty King Mswati III (Makhosetive) presented a keynote speech to the Belgium Government," Dr. Samuel said. "The dinner was very formal, and people were rather stiff. For some unusual reason, protocol was not observed. The hosts asked me to speak after His Majesty. This was most unusual because once the King, as the father of the Nation, has spoken, no other person speaks. But this time they asked me to come forward and say something. I realized that we needed to bring some lightheartedness and camaraderie into the formalities, so I began by complimenting His Majesty's speech for His eloquence, wisdom, and statesmanship. Then I told them he had given a good speech, but I had been privileged to hear Him give the best speech on earth. I told of the day I rushed to the maternity ward at the mission hospital in Manzini to assist a young queen giving birth. Once the baby was born and I lifted the little boy high in the air and smacked his bottom, He gave the best speech He had ever made. This young man declared to the whole world He had arrived, and He was alive and well. The crowd laughed with us heartily, and the atmosphere of the state dinner became a family affair."

"All the while I was travelling with The King, I was still fully operating a medical practice in Manzini. I finally had to send word to His Majesty that I could no longer keep up with the many trips He was taking and with my medical practice in the city as well. With regret I left my position as King's Physician."

Notes

1. Indlovukati (literally, "She-Elephant", pl. *Tindlovukati*; siZulu: *Indlovukazi*) is the SiSwati title for the female head of state of Swaziland and is roughly equivalent to a Queen Mother or Senior Queen in other countries. The title is given preferentially to the mother of the reigning King (styled the *Ngwenyama*, "Lion of Swaziland"), or to another female royal of high status if the King's mother has died. http://en.wikipedia.org/wiki/Ndlovukati, sourced April 2014.
2. *A Little Child Shall Lead Them* can be purchased at www.newhopeswaziland.com or from Amazon as a Kindle book. All proceeds go directly to the home.

9

MISSIONARY LIFE IN AFRICA

Throughout the years that Samuel served Kings, he also focused his life on meeting the needs of the Swazi people. From the beginning, the Hynds' ministry was to be a permanent lifestyle, so the house that Rosemarie and Samuel had built early on in their missionary life was an exciting part of their overall life in Africa. They had plans drawn up for the house. They moulded red, clay bricks and fired them in the swampy valley below the building site. But there was much more to do than build a house.

Samuel, from the time he woke up each day until late at night, spent his days seeing patients, doing surgery, doing postmortem examinations for the government, and testifying in court as to the medical implications of various lawsuits.

Rosemarie joined Anne Stark, another young, missionary wife from Canada, in taking over RFM's X-ray department and helping Kanema with the administrative and financial departments of the hospital. The extra help meant that Kanema could focus more of her efforts on building the Sharpe Memorial Church on the main Mission Station. The Stone Church had become too small to accommodate the congregation, so Kanema set out to build a new church of burnt red brick, which would accommodate more than a thousand people. By building a new church, The Stone Church could now be used for the youth and children's Sunday schools and chapel times. Today it is being renovated to house the museum containing the historical records of the endeavours and passions of the servants of the Lord Jesus Christ in Swaziland.

The Sharpe Memorial Church of the Nazarene in Manzini, Swaziland, built by Rev. Kanema Hynd in memory of her parents to provide for a thousand or more believers each week. It is currently still a place of worship.

Saturdays, for the Hynds, involved going out to the bush to visit former patients and new converts to the Gospel, praying with them, and holding Bible studies to give them encouragement and hope. On Sundays, the Hynds spent their time conducting services, often under a tree out in the bush or in one of the outstation churches. They preached the Word of God and planted new congregations all over the country.

When a bush church, or "wayside church" as they were called, was established, literacy classes would begin immediately so people could learn to read their Bibles. Then parents would want their children to learn and study, so the church building soon served as a school as well. This was the model Kanema Hynd had used in Bremersdorp, starting in her kitchen, moving to the church, and then into a newly built school. As soon as possible, the parents and missionaries would raise funds to build classroom after classroom. Today there are 1,500 primary schools, four high schools, the new Southern African Nazarene University which amalgamates the Bible College in Siteki, the Nursing College, and the Teacher's College in Manzini.

At the hospital, Dr. Samuel worked with experienced medical doctors, Dr. Kenneth Stark from Canada, Dr. Evelyn Ramsey from the USA, and Dr. David, his father. They expanded the clinic work to seventeen rural clinics that were usually built adjacent to a church or a school. In addition, they

Siteki (formerly Stegi) Clinic built for Miss Myrtle Pelley.
She was the first nurse at the Stegi Mission Station.

Some of the churches planted and built
by Rosemarie or Samuel Hynd. Left: Ekuhlamukeni, the first wooden church.

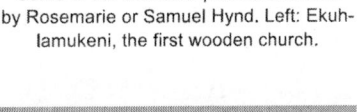

Right: Ekuhlamukeni, replacement
concrete block church.

Left: Ngomane Church,
built of split wood. Later, it
was replaced with a con-
crete block church structure.

taught as lecturers in the Nursing College and expanded the program to include the training of lab and X-ray technicians.

The Nursing College was developed into the leading college of the three British Protectorates: Swaziland, Lesotho, and Botswana. Evelyn Fox, a tutor from the USA, came to teach in the Nursing College. Later she was joined by Ms. Dorothy Davis, also from the USA, who had obtained her graduate diploma as a nursing tutor from the Royal London School of Nursing. This qualified her to be the Principal of the Nursing School. It was her dream to advance the Nursing College to international standards and qualifications within the British Commonwealth. This she did, and she also increased the number of tutors until the annual intake of new students was thirty nurses each year for a three-year course plus a midwifery postgraduate year. The school now offers a full Bachelor of Science degree in nursing as part of the Southern Africa Nazarene University (SANU). Before Dorothy Davis retired, she was awarded the OBE (Order of the British Empire) by Her Majesty Queen Elizabeth II in London for her outstanding achievements.

In postwar years, the Church of the Nazarene became excited about its mission to save the lost, to help those in need, and to relieve the suffering of the sick. Dr. David was the medical superintendent of the hospital and rural clinics. For years, he was also the Head of the Manzini Nursing College, the Manzini Mission Station, and grantee[1] of schools that were being established throughout the country.

During the 1960s while Dr. Samuel was working on refurbishing the hospital with the help of the German and Netherland governments, he was also able to raise funds with them to build a state-of-the-art, double-story high school with classrooms, an amphitheatre assembly hall, and science labs. Manzini Nazarene High is now one of the top academic schools in the country, enabling students to get scholarships all over the world for tertiary education (USA, UK, Australia, and others), and it still regularly wins the annual national all-school choral competitions. It presently serves about 1,200 students. It has prepared many of the current leaders of the Nation with a Biblical/Christian ethic and foundation for life. There are also three other Nazarene high schools: Siteki Nazarene High School, Endzingeni Nazarene High School, and Piggs Peak Nazarene High School. The present Prime Minister is the product of the Endzingeni Nazarene High School. The Teacher's College was moved from the red, brick building of 1953 into a state-of-the-art facility. The original High School and Teacher's Training College buildings became the upper and lower Nazarene Practicing School for student teachers to do their practical work in primary school teaching. It currently has about 600 to 700 students in addition to the original primary school built by Ms. Latta in the 1940s, which also has 700 students.

Manzini Nazarene High School was a state-of-the-art double-story building students moved into in the 1960s. They had been housed in the burnt clay brick building of the 1950s.

God has blessed the entire Nation through those small beginnings in the kitchen's dirt-floored night school, the Old Stone Church's open-spaced school, and the burnt red brick schools. But there is more. It soon became apparent that students enrolling in school had excessive family duties on the

Fine Arts Hall of the Nazarene High School built with funds from the changes in exchange rates.

Right: Nazarene Teachers College built in the 1960s with funds from Germany and the Netherlands.

Left: Original girls' hostel for high school and teachers in training.

New wing of the Student Teachers' Residence Hall built in 1960s with funds from Germany and the Netherlands.

New Residence Hall for Community Health Nursing students built in the 1960s using funds from the Netherlands.

homesteads and could not proceed academically as there was no time for study and no electricity for light to do homework at night. The students needed residence halls where they could live and devote themselves to study. The solution was to build a red brick girls' residence hall on one side of the valley, near where Ms. Parker and the other single teachers lived, and another boys' residence on the opposite side of the valley. One more residence hall was built beside the hospital for Community Health Nursing Students.

*   *   *

In the midst of seeing patients, running out to clinics, and starting wayside churches, Rosemarie and Samuel had their first child: a daughter they named Elizabeth Rose after the baby's two grandmothers, in good Scottish tradition. In those days, babies were born in the Raleigh Fitkin Memorial Hospital with an attending doctor and midwives. Rosemarie had worked all day, and in the evening, she had her first labor pains. She drove herself to the hospital where Dr. David became her attending physician, as her husband was working elsewhere in the hospital.

At 8:00 PM, life for Samuel and Rosemarie took a significant turn, as they became parents for the first time. On the tenth day (post WWII mothers were kept in the hospital for ten days following the birth of a child), the baby and mother were discharged, and the proud dad drove Rosemarie and Elizabeth to the family home. Grandpa David was also thrilled. Every morning after his 4:00 AM devotional and prayer time, he would stop on his way to the hospital to visit and play with his granddaughter before beginning a long day of responsibilities.

Samuel was surprised to see his father doting on his grandchild since Dr. David had been so busy establishing the mission when Samuel was a child. The family saw him when they went out with him to the clinics or wayside churches to work alongside him.

When Samuel married, he made a commitment that he would be sure to take a vacation with his family each year, and he was true to that commitment. Sometimes the Hynd family went to the seaside, since a trip to the seashore was the way in which Rosemarie defined a holiday or vacation. At the beach, the family played in the sand and leapt into the waves of the ocean. Samuel defined a holiday as going to the majestic mountains of Africa where he could ride horses, camp in a caravan or trailer, and feast his eyes on the rugged beauty of God's creation. He loved the grandeur of Champagne Castle and the Cathedral Peaks in the Drakensburg Mountains, the cliffs of the Magaliesburg to the west of Pretoria, or climbing Table Mountain in Cape Town. So at other times, the family would pursue Samuel's dream of a vacation.

The family's first vacation was with Rosemarie's parents to Durban for a seaside holiday. They had just come from England and had their challenges with snakes and creepy crawlies in Swaziland, so they were thrilled to go to a big city and enjoy something familiar—like the ocean.

The next family vacation was to Kruger National Park. This game park is bigger than the whole country of Swaziland and is not far north of Swaziland's border. Elizabeth was just learning to talk and had classified her world into a few simple nouns and verbs, so when she saw the first fur-covered, four-footed animal in the game park, she excitedly hollered, "Kilty, Kilty," and pointed at a giraffe. Kilty was her grandfather David's little black Scottish terrier—a far cry from the towering giraffe nibbling at the top of the thorn trees. The only resemblance it bore to the little dog was that it had four legs and was furry.

Grandpa David's black Scottish terrier dog, "Kilty," and a magnificent giraffe—both were furry and four-legged.

Establishing a home, schools, wayside churches, becoming parents, taking time out for family, working in the hospital, and all the activities in which the family engaged, created a busy life for the Hynd family, but it was also a life full of challenge, learning, and adventure.

Note

1. Grantee of schools meant he was the head of the schools liaising with the government for subventions to help with the teacher salaries and the selection and appointment of head teachers and teachers.

10

FURLOUGH IN THE WESTERN WORLD

By 1957, there were three doctors on-site at the hospital. It seemed to be a good time for the Hynd family to take a year's furlough and travel in North America, Europe, and the British Isles, sharing with churches what God was doing in Swaziland. In this way, churches could be made aware of the huge challenges that needed a great deal of prayer backup for the successful care of the people in Swaziland. Second, the churches could be made aware of the finances needed to support the work of God. Third, speaking in the churches would make folks aware of the opportunities for service if God touched individuals' hearts for Swaziland.

The family flew straight to the USA, stopping only in Labrador, off the Canadian coast, since planes could not fly across the Atlantic in a single flight. They flew into New York City where they stayed with a pastor and his family on Staten Island. Going to the United States through New York City was a delight for Rosemarie. There, she met up with old friends from her days

CHURCH OF THE NAZARENE • AFRICAN FIELD
International Headquarters, 6401 The Paseo, Kansas City, Mo.

Dr. and **Mrs. Samuel Hynd**
Raleigh Fitkin Memorial Hospital
Bremersdorp, Swaziland, South Africa

OUR TASK
to evangelize
126,000,000 pagans
60,000,000 Moslems

OUR NAZARENE WORK
11,000 members
103 missionaries
2 hospitals
21 dispensaries
92,000 patients

PRAY THAT OUR WITNESS MAY BE
FRUITFUL AND FAITHFUL

Preparing the way for visits to churches, schools, and colleges during furlough in 1957.

of training in the United States. For the next twelve months, the family travelled back and forth across the United States and Canada, visiting churches, colleges, and universities. At times, the family travelled together; at other times they split into two teams. They went all over North America. Sometimes little Elizabeth would travel with Samuel as he spoke in churches and at universities around the country. At other times she would travel with her mother for speaking engagements in churches and missionary societies.

The family was in Calgary, Canada, when it snowed during the night. It was the first time Elizabeth had seen snow. She awoke early and climbed up to look out through the window discovering the whole earth was white. She set her parents to giggling and laughing when she called out, "Mummy! Daddy! Come quickly! God has spilt the milk!" Soon she and Dad were out tobogganing in the snow and making snowmen.

The Hynds' furlough was a rich and powerfully transforming experience. During their itineration, they learned that there was a huge family of God who loved them and supported their work in faraway Africa. As they spoke in churches, they

Furlough 1957: Mum and Dad and Elizabeth

saw God stir people's hearts to pray, to give their love by sending letters and gifts, to commit to faithfully support the work
with their finances and to share the great joy of seeing others
hear and know the call of God on their lives.

Visiting Nazarene Colleges that were full of young people
who were alive unto God and ready to serve Him in their lives,
be it in the United States, Canada, Great Britain, Europe, or
Africa, was a highlight.

Some of the heroes of the hour who came to mean so much
in the lives of the Hynd's family members were:

- Reverend Edward Lawlor, the district superintendent
  of Canada. He and his wife faithfully drove the young
  family in their car from church to church across Canada, sharing in the stories, struggles, and triumphs
  the Hynds had encountered on the mission field.

- One unnamed hero was a businessman/farmer from
  a small church in Indiana who heard Dr. Samuel speak
  in the Sunday evening service and went out and
  arranged with the Plymouth car dealership to purchase a black and white Plymouth station wagon. The
  next morning after the service, he called the pastor to
  take the Hynd family to the dealership in town. They
  never met the man who gave them the car that Samuel
  would first use to travel from place to place in the US
  and then as an ambulance in Swaziland. Rosemarie
  would also use it as the family car to take kids to
  school, church, swimming lessons, Girl Scouts, and
  fun family picnics. They shipped the car to Cape Town
  where they picked it up and drove it to Swaziland.

The Lord gave Dr. Samuel some special messages to share
with people all over the world. The first one was about
Lazarus, the man who was covered in sores and sat begging
on the steps of a rich man's house. He told the congregations

that this was the experience of so many people in Africa. Sick and suffering, so many had done the only thing they knew to do, which was to go to the "witch doctor" or *sangoma*.

These *sangomas* are highly gifted and intelligent men and women who serve their communities in times of sickness and distress. Sometimes they use herbal remedies to help those with afflictions, but oftentimes, they use incantations and sacrifices to appease the ancestral spirits, which may have been disturbed in their ancient places, and thus disturb the living. Sometimes these *sangomas* demand exorbitant payments from their "clients," making themselves rich and impoverishing their neighbors in the community.

One such case was a young female *sangoma* who came to see Dr. Samuel. She was very ill with a white man's disease, and she knew she could not treat this condition herself. Dr. Samuel could not help her either. She died and was to be buried not far from her home.

Her twin sister was also a *sangoma*. The funeral service was progressing when mourners began to hear thumping from under the coffin lid. They opened the lid and found the woman was alive. She testified that she had reached a fence with a gate and a wonderful garden beyond. She met people who were on the other side of the fence in the garden. They told her that the only way to enter the garden was through the gate. The only way to go through the gate was through Jesus Christ, but she did not know this Jesus Christ. So now she woke up saying, "Somebody please help me. How do I come to know Jesus? Please help me get all my witchdoctor stuff and destroy it. It must be destroyed because I must repent and make my life right with Jesus."

Everyone was astounded. Samuel and the pastors led her in the prayer of repentance. Then the crowd accompanied her to collect her herbs, throwing bones, clothes, bits of sacrifice animal skins, necklaces, bracelets, paraphernalia, and all the trappings that go with the profession of "witch doctor." She burnt everything and confessed Jesus as Lord. She told her sister she must also repent, be rid of these deceptions and lies. Her sister also burned all of her witch doctor paraphernalia. A few weeks later, the lady died again, suddenly. This time she did not return to life. She was gloriously peaceful when she died and went to Heaven. Her sister continued her walk with Christ, becoming a powerful and effective evangelist and preacher.

This story illustrates the importance of being there to help medically and to provide an alternative of health to the bondage of witchcraft. It is essential to offer freedom from the poverty caused by paying the *sangoma* for needless services and sacrificing to the ancestral spirits. The illnesses encountered in Swaziland needed either the intervention of the miraculous healing power of Christ, or revelations and breakthroughs of medicine. Even when healing came through medicine, there was opportunity to also administer spiritual healing and deliverance from the Swazis' cycle of poverty.

Only the message of Christ brings hope and healing. Swazis had no knowledge of God's love for them. They needed someone to come and tell them that God's Son came to earth to be the Savior of the World. The salvation Jesus brings also brings healing, freedom, peace, joy, long life, and wholeness in every area of life. How could anyone sitting in those services in America not be challenged by the message Dr. Samuel brought? Who could continue doing a regular job of pumping gas at a station or assembling cars when there was a world that needed so much help? Many could not ignore the situations found in Africa and made a commitment to serve the Lord by helping Swaziland.

Another sermon Dr. Samuel preached was based on the idea that when Christ rescues one person, that person will reach others, and soon there will be a Nation of people who know Jesus. In other words, a little one (Swaziland) could grow into a Nation of believers. The tiny Kingdom of Swaziland could become a mighty force for the Kingdom of God. This message astounded North Americans who had a tendency to believe everything was bigger and better in America. Here was a man bringing a message from the smallest country in Africa about how God had "chosen to use the foolish things of this world to confound the wise, the weak things to shame the things that are mighty" (1 Corinthians 1:27, paraphrased).

This little country of Swaziland, nestled in the hills of east Africa, has a profound calling among the nations. In its very beginning, the Word of God came by divine introduction to the King, and he responded and led his people into a relationship with God. It was much like the marriage covenant that was made at Mt. Sinai between God and the children of Israel. In Isaiah 60:22 we read, "A little one shall become a thousand, and a small one a strong nation: I the LORD will hasten it in his time."

Another story Dr. Samuel shared with his American audiences was this one. One day, the staff called him to the hospital. "Doctor, come quickly. A woman is having cardiac arrest in the ward and the attending doctor does not know what to do." There was no ICU or medical equipment to handle such crises. Dr. Samuel rushed to the ward and saw the woman sitting up in the bed, her back arched in agony and screaming. He saw instantly that this was not a medical heart attack but a spiritual attack. As he entered the ward he shouted, "In the name of Jesus, loose her." The demon spirit loosed the woman and she fell back on the bed and rested peacefully. This demonstration of the power of God released a surge of faith in the Swazis as they came to understand about the One who had stilled the waters, healed the sick, raised the dead, and had come to save the World from sin, death, and disease. All the patients in the ward gave their lives to Christ that day as did many others in the hospital who heard what had happened, even though they did not see the miracle.

This deliverance happened to only one woman that day, but through her, many were saved and born into the Kingdom of God. It did not end there. These 80, 100, or 200 people in the hospital had come from places scattered throughout Swaziland. They went home to their neighbors and relatives with the story of the Almighty God and Savior of the world. Then all these communities began Bible studies under the trees at their homesteads, and soon church congregations of born again believers rose up all over the country.

First Corinthians 1:27 tells us that, "God hath chosen the foolish things of the world to confound the wise; and God hath chosen the weak things of the world to confound the things which are mighty." Through the deliverance and healing of one woman, hundreds were born into the Holy Nation of the Kingdom of God, and through them, hundreds and thousands of people all over the country were born again. This is how "a little one shall become a thousand, and a small one a strong nation" (Isaiah 60:22).

In all of these areas where the new churches had sprung up, literacy classes were started. Schools were established to make sure that those who had come to know Christ could study and grow in their faith through reading the Word.

The destiny of Swaziland was set when His Majesty King Somhlolo received and responded positively to the visitation of God. This small Nation becomes mighty as the good news transforms one life, then a thousand lives, and after a while, this Nation becomes the place from which the Word of God goes out to all the Nations of the earth.

The miracle of one life becoming a thousand was repeated again and again in the work of the hospital. People received healing in their bodies, and they also received healing in their souls and spirits. This set in motion a new way of life, a new standard of conduct, and a new freedom from fear and ignorance. Thereby, Swaziland, which had no paved roads (except for a few meters in the capital city) and no electricity when the Hynd family arrived, is turning into a Nation that will bring a testimony of the transforming power of a loving and intervening God.

In recent years, His Majesty King Mswati III has convened meetings of all the traditional kings within the continent of

Africa. His father gave him the name "*Makhosetive*," which means the King of Nations. He is beginning to walk in the prophetic meaning of his name, as he influences the nations of Africa as a leader among kings and presidents and as a speaker of wisdom among parliaments and politicians. Swaziland is becoming the "Pulpit of Africa."

The message Dr. Samuel preached in America gave hope and opened hearts to the call of God. Who would not want to join in this kind of miracle-working enterprise? Where many had felt disqualified from doing missionary work because they weren't preachers or evangelists or because they had not been to Bible College or theological school now saw an open door for anyone who loved God and believed He could use them to reach "one" and that "one" would multiply the one to become "a thousand." Any believing child of God whether he could preach or not could be part of transforming "a small one into a mighty nation."

*   *   *

In 1958, the Hynd family began their journey back to Africa. They first took an ocean liner across the Atlantic to the UK where, once again, they visited churches and attended the famous evangelical Keswick Convention in the beautiful Lake District of Cumbria. They rode the trams in Glasgow and visited longtime friends at the Parkhead Church of the Nazarene. In London, they rode red double-decker buses to visit Dr. Samuel's sister, Isabel, to see Buckingham Palace, and even to go to Windsor Castle. Finally, they turned south and began their journey back to Africa, going overland through Europe by train. When they reached Italy, they boarded a ship that crossed the Mediterranean, passed through the Suez Canal and the Red Sea. Later, the ship sailed the Indian Ocean along the East Coast of Africa, and on down to the southern end of Africa to Cape Town—at the tip of the continent. There they collected their beautiful black and white Plymouth station wagon and drove it home to Swaziland.

The results of their visits to churches in Europe and America bore much fruit: more doctors and nurses came to the hospital, and more teachers came for the teachers' college and high schools. At this time, all the primary school teachers were graduates of the Nazarene Teachers College, as at that time the British Government still maintained the policy that Swaziland was a protectorate and not a colony. Therefore, it still did not provide training for teachers to the Swazis.

The 1961 graduating student nurses and the RFM Hospital Swazi and Missionary servants of God at the entrance of the Nazarene Nursing College.

It soon became evident that the red brick structures built by Dr. David were no longer adequate. The original hospital was plagued by white ants (termites) that were eating their way into the woodwork, the rafters, and the timber doorframes. Even the mud between the bricks was being used up by the termites for their own purposes. Dr. Samuel embarked on a search for a way to renovate and expand the facilities of the mission.

He approached the British Government and others for funds. He found a couple of professional hospital architects in Johannesburg who were Christians. These architects became excited about the vision to restore the hospital and provided their expertise free of charge. They drew up plans in such a way that staff and patients could move easily between the wards, facilities, and supplies throughout the hospital. This improved design meant that the staff would do the least amount of walking and the least amount of contamination of their surroundings.

These were truly exciting, professional times, as the doctors and nurses gathered around and developed a plan. Funding was the greatest challenge, but when God is in something, He is faithful to open bank vaults and pour out resources. The governments of the Netherlands and Germany have a system of taxation that includes funding that is allocated for evangelical and Christian church efforts. So Dr. Samuel, accompanied by the young architects, jumped on a plane, flew to Germany, and then on to the Netherlands to try to work out a funding plan. God had prepared the way before them and gave them favor with the two governments. A few months before the renovation of the Raleigh Fitkin Hospital began; the Manzini Rotary Club gave funds to build a private ward for those who could afford it, rather than having them stay in the open wards crammed with general patients.

There was some opposition to the project from within the church as people were skeptical of the government's involvement. Work proceeded into the 1960s. The evangelical funding from these two countries opened up other opportunities: from Germany came the funds to build a two-story, modern high school for 600 students and from the Netherlands came the funds to build two hostels (residence halls) for students: one for the men and another for the women in training to become teachers. The funds also stretched to build a brand new, two-story, state-of-the-art, teachers training college. The former high school and teachers college buildings were repurposed, forming an upper and lower primary school—the second primary school on the mission. This building doubled the number of children having the opportunity to study. It also served as the practice school for teachers in training. By the 1960s, the mission was a thriving hub of education, healing, and spiritual development.

In 1964, a small primary school was started right at the edge of the Nazarene farm. A missionary lady by the name of Ms. Edna Lochner had been a high school teacher. She was transferred to Manzini and became Superintendent of the Nazarene schools and principal of the Nazarene High School. The two primary schools in the main part of the mission had no more space to accommodate children. Dr. Samuel and Ms. Lochner soon realized that the two schools on the mission were inadequate to house all of the primary school children in the area, so they decided to build another school for an additional 300 to 500 children who could not attend school because there was none in their area. Ms. Lochner's vision, however, was not only to start a school, but also to create a school that would develop and enable its pupils to speak and write English well.

When the school was built, it was constructed on a farm called Beaufort and was named Beaufort Primary School. The land where the school was located was on edge of the

Beaufort Nazarene School, nestled on the Mission Farm to the west of the Nazarene Mission with about 350 students today.

Nazarene farm—right next to the village and yet still on the farm. Dr. Samuel was in charge of the schools. Because he lacked funds, he couldn't put up a proper school at the time. Instead, he built a structure of sticks and mud. After a time the government built a highway through the area, forcing the relocation of Beaufort Primary School. Of course, the mission was compensated for the property the government used to build the highway. That money allowed Dr. Samuel to get a construction company and build a permanent school. It is still in use and is still called Beaufort Primary School. Today the school has an enrollment of 343 pupils with 15 teachers and other staff.

Baby Audrey returns home from hospital with mother, father, and older sister, Elizabeth.

Just a side note about Ms. Lochner. She now lives in Fort Wayne, Indiana. After her retirement she began an organization called Christian Literature for Africa (CLA). At this writing, Ms. Lochner is 90 and is still actively involved in this work. Recently, at a twentieth anniversary for CLA, a retired missionary to Swaziland and Madagascar reviewed the ministry's history. It began in Edna Lochner's living room and to date, has sent almost half-a-million books and Bibles to Africa. Dr. David Hayse, director of Global Literature, expressed his and the Nazarene Church's thanks for Ms. Lochner's years of service. Ms. Lochner, like Dr. Samuel, did not seek a rocking chair upon retirement. They both went on to do great things at an age when many others were ready to sit back and watch the world go by.

In the midst of all this activity, Audrey Grace, Rosemarie and Samuel's second baby girl, was born in RFM Hospital on the Saturday before Easter. Here was a new life, a new character, and a new artist.

11

DR. DAVID PASSES THE BATON

It seemed that sickness and illness took no notice of the calendar. One Christmas Eve, all the missionary families were just sitting down together for a chicken dinner in the lecture hall of the Nursing College. (They'd hidden the skeletons and formaldehyde specimens for the occasion.) Christmas gifts were stacked on the table.

Suddenly a cry rang out and an orderly burst into the room shouting, "*BoDokotela, BoDokotela*! Come quickly! Come quickly! There's a little girl with no leg. A crocodile has eaten it." They learned that a farmer had brought his daughter, Busisiwe (meaning, "we are blessed") Magagula, to the hospital in the back of a *bakkie* (pickup). The girl had been bitten by a crocodile in the Black Mbuluzi River.

Dr. Samuel asked all the other doctors to help him. The doctors ran to collect their white coats from their cars and then rushed to the emergency room of the hospital to find a little girl who had lost so much blood that Dr. Samuel described her as "grey white" under her black skin. All the color had drained out of her. He had never seen anything like this. The leg had been severed cleanly just below the knee. That was fortunate as so often when a crocodile bites it rips the flesh. Quickly volunteers were recruited to give blood to save her life.

The situation was bad but could have been worse. If Busisiwe's leg had been ripped instead of severed, she would have lost even more blood than she had. The doctors dressed

her leg, transfused her, loaded her up on antibiotics, and settled her into the hospital.

Then the doctors learned the whole story. The little girl
had been sent at sunset to collect water from a nearby river.
Fetching water was one of a girl's duties in the Swazi homesteads. As she dipped her container into the muddy water at
the river's edge, a crocodile surged out of the water and

Crocodile

grabbed her leg. The crocodile's means of hunting is
to capture its prey in its
powerful jaws, drag the
prey under the water to
drown it, and then stuff it
in a cave under the water
allowing the flesh to rot a
little and become soft so
the animal can tear off
chunks. Crocodiles do this
because they cannot chew their food but must swallow whole
chunks of meat that they rip off with their powerful jaws.

Busisiwe had grabbed onto the reeds at the water's edge
and screamed for her mother who came running. There was a
huge tug of war with the crocodile. The crocodile wanted to
drown the child, and the mother wanted to save her. The tug
of war raged until the teeth of the crocodile severed the child's
leg. The crocodile swam off with the leg, and the mother
pulled her daughter to safety.

Other children, who had seen what happened, ran to find
their father. He, on hearing about the situation, was fearful for
his children. He jumped on his bicycle and frantically cycled
to a neighboring farm where a white man (Claude Cocket)
lived and begged him to come with his gun and shoot the crocodile. They raced back in clouds of dust in the farmer's *bakkie*
to the river's edge where the father took his dog into the
muddy, swirling waters and pinched the dog's ears to make it
yelp. (Dog is a crocodile's favorite meat.) Sure enough, soon

the nostrils of the crocodile could be seen above the water as it made its way toward the father and the dog.

The farmer aimed his gun at the space between the crocodile's nostrils. The crocodile's hide is full of very strong, thick scales that can cause a bullet to ricochet. However, there is a patch of skin between its eyes where there are no scales. The farmer took aim, the father ducked under the surface of the water with his dog, and the gun blasted. Bull's-eye! The crocodile heaved and belly flopped on top of the water.

The father swam after it, and they were able to drag it to the riverbank and cut open its belly to be sure this was the guilty crocodile. They opened its gut and found the child's leg. Cocket then put the child in the back of his *bakkie,* and they rushed to the Raleigh Fitkin Memorial Hospital about thirty miles (sixty kilometres) away.

The little girl survived and lived with the Hynds for many months while she recovered. Dr. Samuel sought out people and told them her story. These were people who could provide funds for her to be fitted with a prosthetic leg. In those days, all that could be built in Africa was a metal leg with leather straps that was attached to the stump of the leg; but it was better than no leg at all.

Elizabeth and Busisiwe stayed in Johannesburg for some weeks with Elizabeth's grandparents, the Ballards, while the girl was fitted with an artificial leg and taught how to use it. Then they returned to Manzini. The family, the community, and the white farmer were so overjoyed at the amazing rescue, treatment, and survival of this little girl that the farmer gave a piece of his land for a mission to be established. The people rallied to build a church and a clinic, and the whole community came to know the saving grace of God.

A lovely young couple was stationed there and did a marvelous work of grace in that community. Joseph Magagula was a tall, young pastor, and his wife was a bubbly, competent young nurse. She not only established the work of this clinic, but in a few years, she established another clinic on more land given by Suki and Claude Cocket. Remember Claude was the farmer who shot the crocodile.

Lalela Church, pastor's and nurse's home, and clinic where Rev. Joseph Magagula, pastor, and his wife, a nurse, were stationed to serve.

How amazing is the plan of God to save a community through the tragic loss of a little girl's leg and the intervention of persistent caring doctors who would abandon a Christmas feast to save a life. This was the challenge and invitation that Samuel and Rosemarie Hynd presented to people far and wide, wherever they could find an ear to listen.

*   *   *

In 1962, it was time for Dr. David and Kanema Hynd to retire from full-time service. Dr. David passed the baton of service to the Swazi people to Dr. Samuel Hynd. The years of father and son working side by side came to an end. David and Kanema packed up their belongings and moved from the Big House to the doctor's house at the Mbuluzi Leprosarium in the mountains beyond Mbabane.

In 1962 Dr. David and Kanema Hynd passed the baton of service to their son, Dr. Samuel Hynd, and their daughter-in-law, Rosemarie Sylvia Hynd (nee Ballard).

The entire staff gathered on the day of their departure and tied heavy-duty ropes onto their old, black car. As was their tradition of honoring a person, sixteen to twenty men shut off the car and pulled it up the hill from the Big House to the road. Then they pulled it along the road that ran below the girls hostel and above the high school, and then past the primary and practicing schools. They rolled past the football field, the Nursing College, Raleigh Fitkin Memorial Hospital, the Old Stone Church, and out to the main road leading to Mbabane. From there, the David Hynds were allowed to start their car and they departed their full-time, active service to the mission to take up lesser duties at the leprosarium in Mbuluzi. Not only did Dr. David continue his service as a medical doctor at the leper colony, he opened two more rural clinics in the mountainous area beyond the Mbuluzi.

King George VI arrived by train in Goedgegun, the southern town in Swaziland near the Royal residence of Embangweni, to meet with King Sobhuza II. It was here on 25 March 1947 that His Majesty King George VI conferred the honour of Commander of the British Empire on Dr. David Hynd. This was his second honor, as on 11 May 1937 he had been awarded the Order of the British Empire. Goedgegun was renamed Nhlangano, meaning the "Place of Meeting," commemorating this historic meeting of King Sobhuza II, King George VI, and his wife and daughers, including the future Queen Elizabeth Regina II.

Later on he moved to Mbabane, where he saw the need of young people who were jobless, stranded in the city, and living in the streets. He raised the necessary funds from Evangelical Churches throughout Europe to build the Mbabane Youth Centre where young people could live temporarily, receive the

Good News of salvation, and train in woodworking, carpentry, secretarial, sewing, and dressmaking classes.

Meanwhile, Samuel assumed responsibility for the mission's operation, and his family moved from the home built for them in the 1950s into the Big House. Dr. Stark and his family moved into Dr. Samuel's vacated house. Dr. Samuel turned the garage of the Big House into an office to accommodate his duties as Head of the Mission Station. Rosemarie set up her workplace in Dr. David's office that was in the Big House as well, because she had taken on the responsibility of bookkeeping for the mission station and all the schools around the country. Overnight, Dr. Samuel became the Head of the Mission Station, the Grantee of all the schools, and the Medical Superintendent of the hospital and clinics. Fortunately, Mary McKinley came from Ayr, Scotland, to take over the responsibility for the finances of the hospital. Before Dr. David retired, Kanema had been caring for this. Neither Samuel nor Rosemarie had to worry about the hospitals', clinics', or the nursing college's finances. This was a blessing, as their third daughter, Margaret Elaine, named for Samuel's younger sister, arrived on 24 September 1964.

*   *   *

In Swazi culture, a man with three daughters is a blessed man. The third daughter is named "*Thombi Zodwa*," which means "girls only." He is a blessed man because when the girls wed he will receive the *lobola* or dowry—the bride price. The dowry varies with a family's position in society, the family clan or tribe position relative to the hierarchy of power and royalty in the Nation, the beauty of the girl, and the academic achievement the father has assisted his daughter to achieve in life. With three daughters, Dr. Samuel was a very blessed man.

*   *   *

Elizabeth Rose was the first of this "blessed man's" three daughters. She was born on Easter Monday at 8 PM with her

Elizabeth Rose

grandfather Dr. David Hynd as the attending physician. He almost missed the event, though, as he thought that since it was Rosemarie's first delivery, her labor would take time. But Elizabeth was ready to take life into her own hands and was on her way right after supper. Dr. David just made it, thanks to an urgent phone call from Esther Thomas, the attending nurse. She said, "Dr. David, if you don't come quickly you will miss the baby's arrival." By the time Dr. Samuel could get free from his duties and could come to see his firstborn daughter, she was already washed and dressed with a red ribbon in her long black hair. She not only arrived ready for life but she has spent all the days of her life actively involved in community, society, and church, putting her whole heart and soul into anything she deems worthy of her efforts.

Elizabeth started kindergarten when her parents, Samuel and Rosemarie, were on furlough in the United States. The school she attended was on "the loop" in Chicago, Illinois. Later, when they returned from their first furlough, Elizabeth began school in Manzini at the Sydney Williams Primary School. She excelled in her classes all the way through primary school. She competed academically for first or second position with Kenneth, the eldest son of one of the lecturers at the newly formed William Pitcher Teacher Training College (the government teacher training institution) in Manzini. She did not finish primary school in Swaziland, as the Hynd family left in 1965 for their second furlough.

At that time they packed up their home and drove to Durban through a snowstorm in their black and white Plymouth station wagon. Upon arrival, Samuel sold their beloved car to a Christian Indian man before they embarked on the *Africa*, an Italian ship that steamed up the east coast of Africa, stopping in Maputo (then called Laurenzo Marques), Mozambique, Beira, Mombasa in Kenya, Dar es Salam in Tanzania, and up to Aden. From there they proceeded through the Red Sea and on to Port Suez. The trip on the ocean liner was the delight of young Elizabeth's heart. She climbed and explored every part of the ship: the engine rooms, the bridge, and everything in between. She loved swimming in the pool, and by the time the family reached the Mediterranean Sea, she was tanned as brown as a berry. With her golden-brown suntan and long, straight, black hair, she looked more like an Indian child than a girl of Scottish origin.

In Port Suez, Samuel and Elizabeth left the ship and went to Cairo to see the Tutankhamen Museum, to ride on camels across the desert, and to see the pyramids of ancient Egypt. True to her character, Elizabeth insisted she not only had to climb as far up the outside of the pyramid as she could go, but also up the steps inside the pyramid. It was hot and muggy where the stairs were located. When they reached the top, they found nothing but a huge, empty, stone room.

Dr. Samuel and Elizabeth rejoined the ship at Port Said and sailed across the Mediterranean to Venice. Then they took a train across Italy through Bologna and on to Rome to explore the wonders of that ancient city. Elizabeth was especially impressed with the cats that inhabited the catacombs and the amphitheaters where Christians had been martyred and eaten by lions.

The next stop was beautiful Naples where they caught the SS Constitution, an ocean liner, to cross the Atlantic Ocean to New York. What a wonder to come into the harbor and see Manhattan and the Statue of Liberty! The family stayed for an extended time with a pastor's family on Staten Island. They explored New York traffic, the Underground, the Empire State Building, and the United Nations building. All this was fascinating to Elizabeth as she had read so much about New York

in the *National Geographic* and *Time* magazines and in encyclo-
pedias. The Hynds found it exciting to watch this daughter
embrace with enthusiasm, wonder, awe, and curiosity, everything that life presented.

After Elizabeth finished school, she pursued the sciences in
university, though she was also a musician. She studied science
in University of Witwatersrand in Johannesburg, following in
her father's footsteps. She went to Chicago and Nashville in the
United States for her graduate studies before moving into her
calling as a missionary.

She served for three years in Kobe, Japan, following Paul's
missionary style of tent making while spreading the Gospel.
She first worked as an educator in Japan and then moved on
to Hong Kong where she served for twelve years with Jackie
Pullinger, the missionary called to the Walled City of Hong
Kong. (See the book *Chasing the Dragon* by Jackie Pullinger for
an exciting revelation of God at work through the power of
the Holy Spirit.) She learned to live by faith. Later, she was
called to Swaziland by King Mswati III, who confirmed the
call of the King of kings, her Lord and Savior, Jesus Christ.

Elizabeth has been back in Swaziland for twenty years. She
served the Swaziland Nazarene Health Institutions, the Swaziland Christian Health Association, and the Swaziland Bible
Society before God revealed His heart to her about saving
Swaziland. He revealed that He desired to have an "ark" such
as Noah built to save a Nation by rescuing destitute orphan children whose lives were devastated by the loss of their parents,
their homes, their families, and their hope of a future. He
showed her how he desired to bless these children and develop
them into Godly leaders in a Nation ravaged by HIV/AIDS.

Today there are fifty-three healthy, confident, young people, from the age of four to twenty-one, whose lives are demon-
strating that it is God Almighty who "sets the solitary in
families." It is God who is a "Father of the fatherless." It is God
who transforms what the enemy has planned for destruction
into a glorious manifestation of His grace, provision, goodness,

and love through their young lives. Today these fifty-three kids are changing not only their own lives but also the lives of almost 2,000 other orphans throughout the country by leading assemblies in schools, Hope Clubs, and Hope Camps.

*　　*　　*

The second of the blessed man's daughters was Audrey. She was born on Easter Saturday, March 28, shortly after the family returned from their first furlough. Dr. Ken Stark was the attending physician and assisted with an easy and happy delivery of a long, slender, fair-haired, blue-eyed, girl who was to be

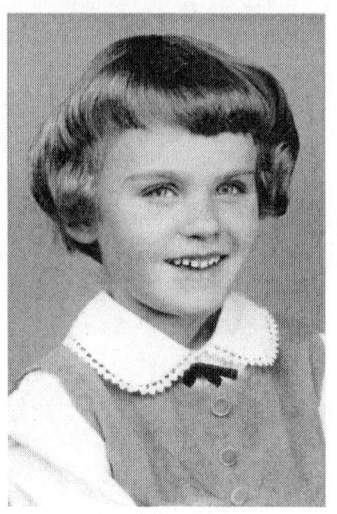

named Audrey Grace—Audrey after Rosemarie's sister-in-law, the wife of her only brother, George Ballard, and Grace after Samuel's elder sister, Isabel Grace, and her grandfather David's youngest sister, Grace. Audrey was different from Elizabeth in every way. She was quiet and reserved and approached life gently and thoughtfully.

Audrey began attending Sydney Williams Primary School with the burden of following in her extroverted sister's steps.

Audrey Grace

Everyone knew Elizabeth. While Elizabeth took the lead role in the school plays and musicals and debates and public speaking, Audrey took the top awards in sports and athletics. While Elizabeth knew no strangers and had friends of every race and language at school and at home, Audrey was more reticent, and her friends were mostly among the missionary children.

Soon Audrey had to go away to school, and as there were a number of missionary children ready for high school, a home called "Farfield" was opened in Pietermaritzburg (near

Durban, KwaZulu-Natal) for missionary children. Various missionary couples from a number of missionary denominations in Southern Africa sent their teenagers to the Pietermaritzburg Girls High or Boys High. Boarding school should have been a good experience for Audrey, but it was not. She and her friends faced many struggles because of the years they spent at this missionary kids' home away from home.

When Audrey graduated from high school, she left South Africa and went to Olivet Nazarene University in the United States. She had her heart set on becoming a missionary nurse to the Native Americans. Audrey only stayed one semester in the United States before returning to her beloved Africa. She found living in the United States was vastly different from life in Africa. She begged and was allowed to return to Africa to study nursing in Pietermaritzburg.

On her way back to Africa, she reconnected with a high school sweetheart. She quickly abandoned her schooling to marry this young man from the Church of the Nazarene in Johannesburg. King Sobhuza II sent several of His wives to grace their wedding in Regents Park in Johannesburg and then escort the young couple to Swaziland for a wedding blessing before the couple established their own home in Ogies, a small town outside Johannesburg.

Here the young couple had their first baby girl whom they named Rosemarie after Audrey's mother. Two years later, Audrey had twins, a boy named Mark who is an artist and lives in England, and a girl named Tracie Anne who is serving as a fourth generation Hynd missionary in Swaziland. She is the early childhood coordinator and alternate director of New Hope Centre in Bethany, Swaziland.

Audrey moved to England for several years, taking the twins with her. The two finished their high school and tertiary years in the United Kingdom. Now Audrey is back in South Africa, living in Benoni just outside of Johannesburg. She is still doing amazing artwork, and, in the family medical tradition, works as a clinic manager in governance.

*   *   *

Audrey was three years old when Margaret (or Margie as she soon was to be called) was born on the evening of 24 September 1964. Margie arrived with a merry heart and an inquisitive mind. She was soon nicknamed Pixie. Margaret Elaine was

Margaret Elaine

named after her father's younger sister, Margaret, and after a missionary's daughter who was loved by all but who had died of the flu a few weeks before Margie was born.

Margie, like Elizabeth, was her own self. With curly brown hair and brown eyes, she entered life ready to explore, investigate, enjoy, and have fun with everyone and everything that crossed her path. She was very young when the family went on furlough, and it was extremely traumatic for her to have her father away from home so much of the time. She had sleepless nights worrying that he would not come back and would not return with the family to Africa. She did not go to school during furlough but spent many hours with her mother doing artwork as Rosemarie was learning to paint. The other girls were in school, so Margie went with Rosemarie to women's Bible studies and prayer meetings.

The World Missions Division of the Church of the Nazarene had a small, wooden-frame house on the Plaza in Kansas City, Missouri, for furloughing missionary families. Rosemarie and the three girls stayed in Kansas City where the girls could go to school while Dr. Samuel travelled by plane, car, train, and bus across the United States and Canada, sharing in churches, at conventions, and at church camps about the mission work he was doing and his vision of caring for the threefold needs of the whole person—body, soul, and spirit. Whenever their dad came to town, Margie would stick to him like glue, riding on his shoulders as he walked and sitting on his lap as he drove the car.

Hynd family photograph taken in Scotland before returning to Africa, 1967.

These furlough days were amazing. The family saw television for the first time. It was exciting, even though it was on an old black and white TV. The timing of their furlough was wonderful. It was at this time that the first manned US spaceship dropped into the Atlantic Ocean. Elizabeth pretended to be unwell so she could stay home from school and watch history in the making.

The family spent little time together after this furlough. Upon their return to Africa, Elizabeth went away to boarding school. The younger girls returned with their parents to Swaziland. Because of what had happened to Audrey at boarding school, Rosemarie was reluctant to send a second child into this environment. It became evident from Audrey's experience that the school she had attended was not the best option for her. The Nazarene Missionaries then set up "One

Way Home" for the teenagers who needed to leave their families to go away to high school. They still studied at Pietermaritzburg Girls High and Boys High, but they lived with couples appointed from among the missionaries to care for them. This was somewhat better, but not the best solution. The best, though unworkable, solution would have been for the girls to be at home with their own parents and attending a local school. It was not possible and so the challenges and scarring of those years happened in Margie's life too. After Audrey left for University in the United States, Margie transferred to Epworth College where her Aunt Margaret, Dr. Samuel's younger sister, had been to school and had excelled as a matriculating valedictorian.

Samuel and Rosemarie, excited to be back in Africa ready to serve, having a lunch break together at home.

Margaret graduated from Epworth College like her aunt Margaret and then went to Cape Town University to study nursing like her Aunt Isabel. She was one of Christian Barnard's team when he performed the first, amazing, historical, open-heart surgery. After several years in Cape Town, Margaret visited her sister Elizabeth in Hong Kong and fell in love with life in that amazingly spectacular city. Hong Kong, often called "The Pearl of the Orient." While there, she decided to further her nursing qualifications by getting her stripes in psychiatry. Becoming qualified required practical work, and as she did not speak Chinese, so she was deployed to the British Military Hospital Psychiatric Unit. The work there was both fascinating and heartrending as most of the patients were Nepalese Ghurkas. These men found the stresses of life in the British army, far away from their mountains and the splendor of life in Nepal, overwhelming. They struggled psychologically.

After Margie completed her qualifications, she did not want to pursue nursing in the military. She was offered a job as a secretary to a wealthy American businessman. While she had no secretarial or business training, she thoroughly enjoyed this work. The management side of her nursing helped greatly in this new job. The businessman sent her for courses in management and administration, and she progressed nicely, though it was vastly different from the socially concerned lifestyle of the Hynd family.

Soon she wanted to be in service to mankind once again. She entered Youth With A Mission's DTS (Discipleship Training Course) in Hong Kong for six months and completed her training in Macau, the Portuguese colony across the water from Hong Kong. Here she worked in an orphanage for six months. Upon completing her training, she continued with YWAM back in Hong Kong where she and another student set up the "Small World Kindergarten" to provide a Christian kindergarten for expatriate and English-speaking people in Hong Kong.

Five years later, she returned to visit her father in Swaziland and went to Living Waters Church of the Nazarene. This was an English-speaking Church of the Nazarene founded by her grandfather, David Hynd, many years before. As the pastor of the church spoke with her, he learned about the Small World Kindergarten she had established in Hong Kong. He begged her to stay in Swaziland and start the same kind of school in Manzini. She prayed about this and thought it might be fun, and so she cancelled her flight back to Hong Kong and re-mained in Swaziland to start the Living Waters Kindergarten.

Living Waters Church and School now serves kindergarten to high-school-aged children.
It began with Margie Hynd in a small room behind the church sanctuary.

Two years later, she moved to the Mbabane Youth Centre, which had been established by her grandfather and father, to begin a Christian preschool in the capital city. It was no easy task living in the Youth Centre as there were many youth in residence who faced challenging situations. How-ever, she persevered and not only started the preschool in the Youth Centre but started and trained teachers for four other Christian preschools.

During this time, her father's friend, Norman Malinga, re-turned from the United Nations where he had been the Am-bassador for Swaziland. He was so impressed with Margie's work that he asked her to consider going back to school for a Bachelor's Degree in Education and returning to establish the Early Childhood College of Education to train teachers for pre-school and kindergarten in Swaziland. She had a full scholar-ship to the University of Natal, so she entered her second

Baccalaureate program in education and not in nursing. Her nursing career was never far from her as she was able to work in nursing homes part-time while she studied education.

Norman Malinga passed away during this time, and the government did not follow through in establishing the Early Childhood Education Centre. Margie returned to Swaziland and found that without Norman Malinga's vision, the plan had fallen through. Even today, there is no government-operated, early-childhood, teacher-training program. The Norwegian Mission and Montessori have started up programs, but still the need is tremendous. Margie, however, had committed herself to Swaziland, and so she worked at Enjabulweni Primary School as a teacher, bringing much life and vitality to its music and drama programs.

However, her heart was not in this, and soon she felt unfulfilled with the regular primary school program. She went to visit her sister, Audrey, in England and found a teaching post in London. The working conditions and school environment of education in the United Kingdom were vastly different from Africa. After she completed her two-year commitment, she left education to reenter the medical world of nursing. She soon found a husband and married. They had a son, named Stephen John, who did well in primary school and showed his brilliance at chess, even though he was still very young. Today, they live on the Isle of Wight, just off the southern coast of England.

*   *   *

Through these years of family growth, Dr. Samuel and Rosemarie's lives were full and rich. The renovation of the hospital, nursing college, teachers' college, high school, and residence halls for students brought the community into a new place. Many new missionaries, national workers, and graduating Swazi students started to take up positions in the schools, churches, clinics, and the hospital. The Manzini Mission Station became a very busy, vital hub of liveliness.

The team of Swazi workers grew. There were missionary doctors, nurses, lab technicians, teachers, and lecturers from places such as, the Philippines, the United States, the United Kingdom, South Africa, Australia, Canada, and Swaziland.

Photo of the missionary family in 1967, taken in front of RFM Hospital with the original arches built by Dr. David.

As Head of the Mission, it was Samuel's responsibility to serve the "family" of ever-increasing workers as a father figure and chairman of the leadership committee. This sort of work included the challenge of fighting bush fires on the mission farms that supplied milk, yogurt, beef, *mielie* meal, and vegetables for the hospital patients, the nursing students, the teachers training college students, and high school students living within the mission.

Samuel's duties included leading the Saturday night prayer and praise meeting for all the missionaries each week. He and Rosemarie happily hosted any visitors from the leadership of the Church of the Nazarene who came to visit. What a blessing of foresight on his mother's part to build the Big House for family, friends, prayer meetings, gatherings, and visitors from far and wide.

12

A TRAGIC ACCIDENT

On 1 January 1972 at around 5 PM, a freak accident turned life upside down and inside out for Samuel and his three daughters. It happened in the driveway of the family home. Dr. David and Kanema had come from Mbabane on New Year's Day to enjoy the day with the family. Isabel, Dr. Samuel's sister was with them, as she was visiting for the Christmas holidays from England. At around 5 PM, they were ready to go home, and Isabel was going to drive the elder Hynds back to Mbabane.

The day before, Rosemarie had packed her younger daughters' suitcases because the family was going on a short vacation before taking the girls to the Missionary Children's Home in Pietermarizburg to start the new school year on January 8th. The suitcases were packed and ready, and the girls would be leaving in the morning with their parents.

Isabel got into the car to ready herself for the drive back to Mbabane. Earlier, Dr. David had moved the car from where he had parked it in the shade to a place beside the lawn to make room for the kids to ride their bicycles around the driveway. When he got out of the car, he switched off the engine but left the car in reverse gear. Rosemarie was assisting her mother-in-law, Kanema, into the back seat of the car, and Isabel was in the driver's seat. She was accustomed to driving an automatic car, so she did not press the pedal to engage the clutch. When she turned the key in the ignition, the car jumped into reverse gear knocking Rosemarie off her feet. She fell backward over an embankment, and the car plunged off the edge of the driveway as well. The car went sideways, crashing onto the rocks, and pinned Rosemarie between the car door and the body of the car, with all the weight of the car on her. She was trapped. She cried out, "Isabel," and then was silent.

Dr. Samuel was at the hospital that afternoon clearing his desk in preparation to leave the next day with his family on vacation and then on to school. Audrey and Margie were playing with the other missionary children at the tennis courts. Elizabeth had gone back to her summer job in Johannesburg. A horrified Dr. David Hynd stood at the front of the car and watched the tragedy unfold before his eyes. He called Samuel at the hospital and told him to come quickly. When the phone call came, Samuel rushed from the hospital to his home, where he found his mother, father, and sister totally distraught and standing beside the vehicle that still pinned Rosemarie's body to the ground.

She had died instantly. She hadn't even bled. She looked perfectly fine, except that her lungs and organs were crushed. As a doctor, Samuel fell on his knees in the dirt and began to examine the injured patient—his beloved wife—who was now silent and still. His fingertips found the jagged edges of the broken ribs that had punctured her lungs. He knew it was too late, and he began to stroke her head. Someone asked a farmer to bring a tractor to pull the car off her body. Once she was freed, they laid her in the back of the station wagon and took her to the mortuary at the hospital. She was DOA (Dead On Arrival).

Family and friends began arriving as word got out. Soon the house was full of loved ones, but for the family, everything seemed hollow, and every conversation sounded as if it were an echo from some faraway place. Swazi loved ones came in groups of twos, threes, fives, twenties, fifties, and more to gather and "cry" with the family. The Swazi custom was to come and share love and appreciation for the lost loved one. They offered encouragement from the Word of God that came directly from their hearts along with songs, psalms, and prayers.

For days, the other missionaries and townspeople provided meals for the many people who came from near and far.

They had to plan and prepare for the funeral, and yet, everyone walked and talked like men frozen in a forest. Everyone walked in a fog of shock, disbelief, grief, and trauma.

After the shock subsided, grief started. "If I had just done this, this might not have happened," Dr. Samuel tried to reason. "If my father had not left the car in gear . . . If my sister had only remembered the clutch. . . . My poor sister. It took five years for her to get over it. I felt so sorry for her. It wasn't her fault."

Margie retreated to her room to play with her dolls. When she was found, she was singing to herself, "Because He lives I can face tomorrow, because He lives all fear is gone. Because I know, I know, He holds the future, and life is worth the living just because He lives."

Audrey was in the garden with her guitar playing a version of Psalm 23 that had been written by Ralph Carmichael and sung by Cliff Richards, "Because the Lord is my shepherd, I have everything that I need. He lets me rest in meadows green and leads me beside the quiet stream . . . Even when walking thru the dark valley of death, valley of death, I will never be afraid, for He is close beside me, guarding, guiding all the way . . . His goodness and unfailing kindness shall be with me all of my life, and afterwards I will live with him . . . forever in His home."

Rosemarie's girls chose to sing these songs as their testimony at the funeral. The mission men came forward and sang the Bill Gaither Trio's song, "The King is coming, the King is coming, praise God, He's coming for me."

The funeral was held Saturday, 4 January, at 11 AM, and it lasted until 5 PM. It was a day of relating wonderful stories of God at work through the life of one woman who had lived at peace with all persons, who was loved and treasured by all, and who had no enemies because of her deep love for Her Lord and Savior and her fellow man. She had led Bible studies with the Emakhosikathi (King Sobhuza's forty-five wives) in their various Royal residences. She had been an active participant and leader in the Women's Fellowship meeting on Wednesday afternoons in the Old Stone Church. She had started several churches out in the rural areas and, most recently, had been working to establish a church at Maliyaduma, in the hills to the east of the city of Manzini, where she had also started a wayside Sunday school class under a tree next to a former patient's homestead—a patient who had been born again while in the RFM Hospital.

"I had never seen a funeral like this one," Dr. Samuel said. "The church was so full that, at one point, Dr. David told those who had been sitting for the first few hours to go outside and let the folks outside come in for the rest of service. The British High Commissioner was there, and he said he had never been in such a long service in his life. Everyone wanted to talk. Everyone wanted to give tribute to the life of Rosemarie Sylvia Hynd (nee Ballard)."

Church leaders from around the world flew in for the funeral. Brother James Graham, a Nazarene missionary, came down from Malawi where he was stationed. Rosemarie's parents had passed on the year before the accident, and only her brother, George, his wife, Audrey, and their three sons living in Montreal, Canada, were the immediate family left. The distance and cost were too great, so they could not come for the funeral. Missionaries and church leaders gathered as did the chiefs, pastors, friends, and families from all over southern and eastern Africa. Dr. David read the obituary, sharing how wonderfully kind, loving, and helpful in every way, his only daughter-in-law, Rosemarie, had been to him. She had also been a loving wife to Samuel and a wonderful mother to her children. She was a loyal and loving friend to all who came her way.

"We fed more than 1,700 people a belated lunch." Dr. Samuel remembered with great tenderness, "At sunset we put the coffin carrying the love of my life, my best friend, and fearless prayer warrior in the back of my green Chevy station wagon and drove up the hill to the small mission graveyard where our dear friends Ken and Anne Stark's son was buried, and also Reverend and Mrs. Wise's teenage daughter, Elaine, after whom our youngest daughter was named. Rosemarie's mother, Lily, and her father, Stan Ballard, were buried there as well. There was not even a headstone on their graves. We stood under a huge, old mango tree and sang in English and SiSwati of our hope and trust in the Almighty God whom we loved and served in this land.

"It was past sunset and darkness was closing in as we took handful after handful of dirt to throw on our beloved Rosemarie's coffin," Dr. Samuel continues. "Dust to dust, and we laid her body to rest. We rejoiced that her soul and spirit were now fellowshipping with the saints who had gone before us, and the whole crowd of witnesses and the heavenly hosts rejoicing and praising God in the glorious peace and joy of life in Heaven. As day closed into darkness and life closed into a treasury of memories, we remembered the words of an old song, 'Only one life, twill soon be past, Only what's done for Christ will last.'"[1]

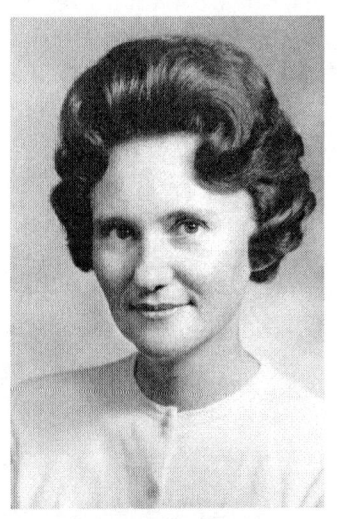

Rosemarie Hynd

It is interesting to remember how God had led Rosemarie in her last days. She had been honored to be godmother to two of the children of the Zulu king, King Zwelethini, as she had been a very close friend to Princess Manthombi, the Swazi princess who had married the Zulu king. For ages, the Royal family had invited her to come on a state visit to Zululand to visit with the children, instead of the children visiting with her when they came to Swaziland. In September, at the time of national independence celebrations in Swaziland, Rosemarie was moved with urgency to make the state visit to Zululand happen. She was escorted south to the Lundi area in Zululand as the Royal guest of the young princess and prince.

Another evidence of God's leading was a celebration Rosemarie held on Boxing Day just before the accident. The Hynd family always celebrated their Christmas dinner and gifts in the cool of the evening on Christmas Eve (Christmas comes at the height of summer in the Southern Hemisphere.) Christmas Day was always a celebration of giving to others for the Hynd family by going out to the outstations. When they came home on Christmas Day, they were happy, content, but too tired to even think of making food or giving and receiving their own gifts. In the weeks leading up to Christmas, the Hynd family would busily search for clothes, toys, and anything else that could be found and wrapped up as gifts. The gifts were taken to the outstations so that every child in the community who came to the church to celebrate the birth of the King of kings would have a gift representing the wonderful gift of God, our Savior and Lord, Jesus, God's only begotten Son.

It had been Rosemarie's dream, for a long time, to invite everyone she loved to her home for a Boxing Day feast. Boxing

The site of the accident where Rosemarie Hynd was crushed under the weight of a car on 1 January 1975.

Day, 26 December, had always been special to her. It is the day in Europe when families pack up any extra food they have from their Christmas Day feast and they share it with their neighbors, friends, and especially any poor amongst them. It is a traditional time of visiting and sharing. This year she decided she would do what she had always dreamed of doing. When she returned from visiting the Zulu prince and princess, she began making arrangements for a huge party. She had a God-given urgency.

She arranged for hundreds of friends to come, visit, and have lunch with the family at the Big House. She arranged for a cow to be roasted on rocks in a pit to supply the visitors with choice beef. People began arriving at around 11 A.M, and when all was done at about 5 P.M, Rosemarie was happy and content. Neither she nor anyone else knew that within one week she would be feasting and partying with all the saints in Heaven whom she had loved and who had loved her. Life on earth was almost over.

*   *   *

As they left Sharpe Memorial Church after the funeral, the local Catholic priest gave an offering of one-hundred Rand to start the building fund for the Rosemarie Sylvia Hynd Memorial Chapel to be built at RFM Hospital. It took a while, but sometime later, the chapel was built at the hospital.

Eileen Figge, former missionary nurse and lecturer at the Nazarene Nursing College, was the glue that kept the Hynd family together through those hours and days. She made sure meals were served and people were welcomed and sent off. For days and weeks, people came with love and tears, bringing words of comfort, encouragement, and praise for the goodness of God because He had shared His precious daughter with them for more than twenty years in Swaziland.

Dr. Samuel, his three children, two sisters, and parents went to Durban for a couple of weeks together before Audrey and Margie had to begin boarding school in Pietermaritzburg.

Samuel's sister, Isabel, went back to her life in the United Kingdom. His younger sister, Dr. Margaret, and Elizabeth returned to South Africa. Elizabeth went back to her studies in university.

Rosemarie Hynd Memorial Chapel at the entrance to the Manzini Nazarene Mission adjacent to the original stone house (to the left) and the new administration block of RFM hospital (to the right).

Life for Dr. Samuel resumed in a big empty house with five bedrooms, three bathrooms, a dining room, living room, kitchen, and two offices. Those weeks and months are dull in his memory. However, God gave Samuel grace so that he could continue in ministry and in serving people and patients. As Corrie ten Boom said, "The measure of a life, after all, is not its duration, but its donation." So Dr. Samuel went on giving of himself to meet the needs of the Swazi people.

There was no way he could continue with a full plate of responsibilities. "I was totally devastated. I was distraught," said Dr. Samuel. "It was like something had hit me, and I didn't know what I was doing. Then I read a book that told me how to deal with my devastation. It helped me some."

With the death of his wife, Dr. Samuel felt as if his life had been amputated from his very being. The Psalms of King

David became his constant companion and comfort, as never before in his life. He stepped out from his involvement in the district and church outreach work and focused on his medical and Head-of-the-Mission work. Then, after a year, the Swazis and elders came and told Dr. Samuel, "You can't stay like this. You need a wife." Of course, people had several candidates in mind for him to marry.

"I thought of all the candidates here. It wouldn't be easy to satisfy everybody with my choice. But I knew Phyllis Mc-Neil, and she was a nice girl who was committed to what she was doing. She had been a good friend to Rosemarie so she knew me, my desires, and what I would like. I asked her to marry me and she accepted." But Dr. Samuel did not tell his daughters—yet.

Phyllis was a missionary nurse from Kansas with a degree from Bethany Nazarene University. She had a call to missions, and when the mission headquarters assigned her to Swaziland, she went first to Glasgow, Scotland, for one year's training in midwifery. Dr. Samuel, as Head of the hospital, had introduced the policy of US missionary nurses doing a graduate year of midwifery training in the United Kingdom or in South Africa to qualify them for registration with the Government of Swaziland. Because he had trained in Scotland, it was easy for him to set up a program of midwifery training for US nurses in Glasgow hospitals and at the midwifery college.

During her midwifery training, Phyllis had made friends with many of Samuel's Scottish friends. When she came to Swaziland, she had been very active in medical and church activities. Eventually she became the Principal of the Nazarene Nursing College. She was no stranger to Samuel and the work he was doing in Swaziland.

*   *   *

In October of that year, Dr. Samuel was due for a furlough. So he and his two younger girls went by air to London and visited family and friends on their way to the United States and the

Church of the Nazarene Headquarters in Kansas City. Elizabeth was completing her exams at University so she followed the family later. She flew first to Columbus, Ohio, where she stayed with Eileen Figge's mother until Dr. Samuel completed his preaching services nearby. Then he collected her and they joined the two younger girls who had been staying with former missionaries, Chuck and Marty Howard, in Ashland, Ohio.

Then, when they were all together, Dr. Samuel shared with his daughters that he was going to marry Phyllis McNeil, the principal of the Nazarene Nursing College in Manzini. That was only part of the shock of his announcement. He told them that Phyllis was already in the United States getting ready for their wedding, which was to be held in Kansas City on Saturday, 3 January, 1976. The girls, who had been away from home all that year doing their schooling, had no idea of their father's new relationship. They were stunned.

Dr. Samuel and the girls drove to Montreal, Canada, to be with Rosemarie's brother, George Ballard, and his family for Christmas. It was cold for those who were used to living in Southern Africa. After Christmas, they drove south to Kansas

Samuel and Phyllis Hynd begin a new life together.

City for the wedding. On a cold, wintery day at the Nazarene Theological Seminary chapel, Dr. Samuel Hynd and Phyllis McNeil began their life together.

After the wedding, the girls flew to Los Angeles to stay with some of the retired African missionaries at Casa Robles, the home for retired Nazarene missionaries from around the world, giving the newlyweds time for a brief honeymoon. Samuel and Phyllis joined them at Casa Robles for a short family vacation visiting Disneyland and Hollywood, before the girls had to head back to Africa to begin school for the next term.

Note
1. Written by C.T. Studd, 1860-1931.

13

A NEW LIFE

Life was never to be the same. Upon their return to Swaziland, Dr. Samuel and Phyllis found all of the family's belongings had been stored in two rooms and all the other rooms had been emptied. Russell and Ruth Human had taken up the responsibilities as Head of the Mission Station and were living in the house. Shortly thereafter, major changes occurred politically in the Kingdom, and Dr. Samuel entered into a new life of serving the people of Swaziland.

Swaziland had obtained independence from the British in a peaceful handover on 6 September, 1964. King Sobhuza II had been reinstated as Head of State with a British style parliament of two political parties, but this arrangement had not gone well in a small Nation of one tribe, one people, and one family. In 1972, the King rescinded the parliamentary system and suspended all political parties. A new form of government had to be birthed—one man and one vote without political parties. A transition was necessary.

During the last years of British rule, Dr. Samuel had been the King's (Paramount Chief's) physician, and when His Majesty King Sobhuza II was reinstated, Dr. Samuel became the Royal Physician. "One night a police officer came to my house. He said, 'Come with me.' I thought someone in the Royal family must be sick, so I gathered my medical bag to go help.

"The police officer took me to the Senate House. There I found five other men. I asked, 'Well, what are you doing here?' They said, 'A policeman came to our door and told us we were to be here.' None of us had any idea why we had been summoned. The policeman said, 'If you need to go to the toilet, you can't go alone. You have to have a policeman go with you.'

"We were then called one by one from the Senate House into the hall. We still did not know why we had been summoned. I walked in and was told I must stand. I was not to say anything, just to stand there. After a while, someone announced my name and who I was. Then I was taken to the library. There was a man with a camera and a chair. He said, 'I will take your picture—just like your passport picture.' So they took the picture, and I was taken back to the Senate House. By this time there were twenty or more of us, and it was then we found out that we were candidates for elections to parliament. When we were all finished, we were not to tell anyone why we had come there. That wasn't difficult because we still didn't know what was going on.

"The next day, I was doing surgery in Mbabane Clinic, and at midday, I went to town to find some lunch. Someone stopped me and said, 'Congratulations!' I said, 'Thank you, but what for?' He said, 'You got the second highest votes by the electoral college. You are in parliament.' I said, 'What? I didn't know that.' He said, 'Well, didn't you hear it on the radio this morning?' I answered, 'No, I don't listen to the radio at six o'clock in the morning.'

"We learned that those of us who were elected would be called. After three weeks, we took the oath of office and were sworn in with the Bible. Then we were allowed to go on with life. A few weeks later, I was on my way to get lunch in Mbabane, once again, when a man stopped me in the street and said, 'Congratulations!' Again, I thanked the stranger and asked, 'What for?' He said, 'You are the Minister of Health.' Another three weeks passed, and I was sworn in as the Minister of Health.

"It was then that I learned a terrible word, 'bureaucracy.' I also learned that there was a brand new Parliament and a brand new government—it was a trying time. When you tried to bring about change, the answer would be, 'It can't be done' or 'We have never done it that way.' It was very frustrating."

As Minister of Health, Dr. Samuel had to move into a government house in Mbabane, the capital city. There, Phyllis set

up a family home and equipped it for entertaining. Those years involved many public events and service to the Nation. Phyllis focused her talents and abilities on establishing the Manzini Medical Centre. She was an excellent manager and set up the clinic with general consulting rooms; the Queens' consulting room (the wives of King Sobhuza II, were all cared for privately in the clinic); a waiting room; a simple laboratory; an X-ray and film developing room; and a maternity unit. (It was in this maternity unit several years later that several of His Majesty King Mswati III's children were born.)

Dr. Hynd as Minister of Health.

Dr. Samuel continued to practice in his Manzini office near the George Hotel two days a week while serving in the Cabinet full time. This way he was able to maintain the medical care of individuals while managing the health care of the entire Nation. Dr. Zwane, a young lady doctor who had trained in Scotland, worked full time with Phyllis and Dr. Samuel during his five years of Cabinet service.

After his years in government, Dr. Samuel returned to full-time, medical work in Manzini, with Phyllis working alongside him until she began to find the stress of managing the clinic too taxing. Audrey's childhood friend, Mollie Lourens, a qualified RN, joined the team and took over management of the clinic.

Phyllis' parents came to visit, and she saw that her father was ailing. Not long after her parents returned to the United States, she decided to go to there for a short time to be with her father as he struggled with his health. Unfortunately, her father passed away before she could get through snowstorms and other delays in the United States. Dr. Samuel tried to fly over for the funeral, but as it was the Christmas season and the airlines were overbooked, he was unable to get a flight in time for the funeral.

Manzini Medical Centre opposite the George Hotel in the centre of town became a historic place as King Mswati III's firstborn entered life on earth in the small maternity ward.

Phyllis returned to Swaziland and, shortly thereafter, learned that her mother, who had moved in with her sister after the passing of Phyllis's father, was rapidly deteriorating. Her sister called Phyllis to come home as there was not much time left for their mother. She went once again to the United States, and in a short time, her mother died. At nearly the same time, Phyllis was diagnosed with trans-ischemic attacks (TIA) and was not allowed to fly due to the risk of death that could be caused by changes in air pressure on planes. It was sad that her health deteriorated rapidly also. She remained in her sister's care until she too passed away in Louisiana, where her sister and brother-in-law pastored a Church of the Nazarene.

*   *   *

Again, Samuel faced life without a helpmate. However, God had provided a home for him on the outskirts of the city of Manzini. Years before, when Rosemarie's parents had come from England to meet their first granddaughter, Elizabeth, they had decided to stay in Africa and be close to the family. They had purchased a lovely cottage on the Elwandle Road overlooking Manzini from the eastern side of the hills surrounding the city. They bequeathed this house to Rosemarie, and she willed it to her spouse, Dr. Samuel. After his years in service as Minister of Health, he moved to this house, and it became his permanent home.

Dr. Samuel's days began early at 6 AM with breakfast and ended most days after midnight. People often asked him how he managed the load that came with political, medical, and community responsibilities. His response was always, "Every morning I drive out of my home along the ridge overlooking the city from the eastern side, and I thank God that I am alive. I thank God for every person He will bring into my life that day those I can help, serve, and to whom I can bring comfort and hope. By the time I reach the city and begin the day, be it in a Cabinet meeting, seeing patients, or meeting with His Majesty and His Cabinet ministers, I am full of thanksgiving that brings the fullness of joy and the strength of the Lord. It is sufficient for the day. My joy in service has always been my strength."

14

COMMITMENT TO
THE NATION

He embraced the Living God.
He embraced the Nation.
He loved a people.
He served unceasingly.
He searched for a city,
whose architect and builder
was the Lord God of Heaven and earth.
ELIZABETH HYND

The saying goes like this, "You pray like everything depends on God, and you work like everything depends on you." One of Dr. Samuel's favorite scriptures is found in Proverbs 3:6 is: "In all thy ways acknowledge Him, and he shall direct thy paths." Another verse is 2 Corinthians 12:9: "My grace is sufficient for thee: for my strength is made perfect in weakness," and yet another is 1 Peter 1:7: "That the trial of your faith, being much more precious than gold that perisheth, though it be tried with fire, might be found unto praise and honor and glory at the appearing of Jesus Christ" (KJV).

The life of Dr. Samuel Hynd has been one of serving God with all his heart, all his might, and all his understanding. He says, "I truly thank God that he has sustained me all these ninety years since conception," (he chuckles), "and I have been healthy and strong. In school, I was an athlete, excelling in the high jump, sprinting, the long jump, cross-country running, field hockey, and tennis. This has kept me fit and strong." His children tell of a day they were driving through the bushveld near Hhelehhele when some young herd boys hurled stones at the moving car from an embankment. Dr. Samuel stopped the car, ran after them, caught them both, and marched them off to the chief's residence where he requested they be disciplined for inappropriate behavior. His girls say it never paid to try to run away from him because he could always run faster than they could.

He has only had two challenges in his health all these years: once, not long after struggling with all the adjustments of losing Rosemarie, he found himself in hospital for an emergency surgery because of bleeding ulcers. They had to remove a third of his stomach. A second challenge happened one day in Johannesburg when he had a gall bladder attack while shopping in a huge wholesale store called Makro (somewhat like Sam's Club in the United States), and he was rushed to Kenridge Catholic Hospital for emergency surgery. In spite of working with sick patients and extensive hours each day in many different roles and responsibilities, the Lord has been his strength and shield, supplying His grace and strength sufficient unto the day.

A guiding principle of his life came from his father: to serve mankind, one must serve with body, soul, and spirit. In all his ways, Dr. Samuel has endeavored to do such. His first love is the health and prosperity of the body, the temple in which a person lives, for without this temple there is no place for the soul and spirit of a man to dwell in order to manifest the glory of God on earth. Dr. Samuel says, "God has led me to so many different places and has given me so many opportunities to serve that I can only rejoice in His goodness toward me, for I have been, and I am, honored and blessed."

Minister of Health

"My highest honor as a medical doctor, as a citizen of Swaziland, and as a servant of the Most High God was the honor of serving as the Minister of Health in the Kingdom of Swaziland. This enabled me to embrace the Nation's health," says Dr. Samuel with a faraway look in his eyes.

Serving under two prime ministers as Minister of Health, Dr. Samuel was responsible for all the doctors, nurses, hospitals, and clinics, and rather than overseeing the health of only the city of Manzini from his home and clinic, he now oversaw the entire Nation of Swaziland from the capital city of Mbabane.

As Minister of Health, the leprosarium was under his care. When it closed, he was able to negotiate for the colony to be used as a training facility in nutrition and food production, and he became the head of that training program.

Hoof and mouth disease came and went for the livestock in Swaziland, resulting in severe challenges for an agrarian culture that uses cattle as its measure of wealth and investment. While Dr. Samuel was Minister of Health, there was yet another outbreak of hoof and mouth disease, and he used this tragedy as an opportunity to boost the entire agricultural industry in the land. As was required by the veterinary health laws, an area struck by hoof and mouth disease had to be physically quarantined. There could be no transport of livestock from the diseased areas into the clean areas. Dr. Samuel, as Minister of Health, closed the borders of the country and did not allow any cattle to be transferred across international borders. No cattle in and no cattle out unless you had a permit that your cattle were clean.

"I was not very popular at that time," he said. In addition to closing the border to livestock, he also closed it to all produce. He did this because Swaziland had become dependent on South Africa for imports of vegetables, fruits, poultry, milk, beef, and so on. By closing the borders to all forms of produce, he was able to force the revitalization of the agrarian communities of Swaziland. Food and nutrition had to come from the local farmers, and this meant that the local economy and commerce were given an enormous boost. Today in Swaziland there is a full-quota poultry industry, and the country is approaching a full quota in milk production. There is, however, still great opportunity for Swaziland to provide all the produce needed by its people. Swaziland has wonderful soil and plentiful rain. The Chinese Agriculture Mission in Swaziland is able to raise three crops of rice per year, beating anything they are able to raise in Taiwan. More can be done to provide the country with produce.

Immunizations were part of the health care system. When Dr. Samuel came to the country as a small boy, people died of treatable diseases like malaria, amoebic dysentery, typhoid, and the like. They also suffered from smallpox, polio, leprosy, and other diseases. Independent Swaziland, as part of the World Health Organization, was able to manage immunizations countrywide. All vaccinations were introduced at world-class standards through the clinics and were administered free of charge, but many people did not come for these immunizations. All babies were to receive immunizations, but many were not born in health facilities and so were left out of the treatment programs.

As Minister of Health, Dr. Samuel was also a member of the World Health Organization (WHO). "In our WHO meetings," he said, "we discussed the degree of infections in the world and what we had to do to counteract them. We tried to cover the nations and especially the children. WHO helped supply drugs in a limited fashion."

A plan of action was necessary, and divine inspiration was needed. Dr. Samuel envisioned an Integrated Health Service for Swaziland. Once, when returning to Swaziland from a WHO conference in Geneva, Switzerland, Dr. Samuel stopped in Nairobi, Kenya. He went to see their hospitals and systems of staffing. "I was well hosted, and I saw a lot of what I needed to learn. This information became valuable in making changes in Swaziland."

The changes he made led to the integration of the entire health service of the country. First of all, health care needed to be tiered with primary, secondary, tertiary, and specialist care. The Mbabane Government Hospital was designated as the referral hospital of the nation so that services, which were specialized, costly, and limited to fewer cases, could be dealt with in Mbabane. Any conditions, treatments, or surgeries that required specialist surgeons or physicians above the capacity of the national hospital in Mbabane were to be referred into the South African referral system. His Majesty King Sobhuza II set up a fund to make it possible for people to be able to go for services not available in Swaziland. For example, kidney dialysis, MRIs, specialized scans, and surgeries were covered in South Africa.

The next level was regional referral hospitals. In the Hhohho Region (northern region of the country), the Piggs Peak Government Hospital with 150 beds, was designated as a referral hospital. In the Lubombo region (in the eastern mountains), the Good Shepherd Catholic Hospital was so designated with its 150 beds. In Shiselweni (the southern region where the first Methodist missionaries began), the Hlatikhulu Government Hospital, with its ninety beds, was also designated. In the Manzini Central region, the RFM Hospital, with its 350 beds, was integrated into the national scheme of health care. The eighteen Nazarene primary health care centres or rural clinics, the Anglican clinic in Luve, and the Swedish Free Evangelical mission hospital in Emkhuzweni to the north were all integrated with the other mission and government clinics into the government plan. The objective was that no patient would need to travel more than a few miles from his or her homestead to receive treatment. The cost of this medical care was worked into the national budget rather than through the budgets of mission hospitals and clinics. In that way, health care could be developed and maintained throughout the Nation. The integrated health system of government hospitals, mission hospitals, and clinics was one of Dr. Samuel's greatest contributions to the health of his Nation.

Before Dr. Samuel became Minister of Health, he had cared for the Royal family as Royal Physician. This continued throughout his term as Minister of Health. After his term of office, he continued as private physician to King Mswati III when He was crowned King of Swaziland.

As Cabinet Minister, Dr. Samuel lived in Mbabane, but every Tuesday, the cabinet spent the day at Ludzidzini, the Royal Residence in the Lobamba area, meeting with the King to discuss and debate national affairs, while Fridays were allocated for public functions. The King often required His cabinet to accompany Him in His public duties of officiating at the opening of hospitals, clinics, schools, or even the annual trade fair in Manzini.

Dr. Hynd accompanying Young King Mswati III at the Manzini Trade Fair. Dr. Samuel was Minister of Health at the time.

Dr. Samuel was also required in Parliament and administered the national affairs of health through his Principal Secretary, Under Secretary, Chief Medical Officer, Chief Nursing Officer, and the team of civil servants in the Ministry of Health. He managed to continue his medical practice a few days a week in Manzini with the help of Dr. Zwane, Phyllis, and his nursing staff, during his years in office. During this time, Dr. Samuel was also instrumental in bringing more service providers into the country such as the Salvation Army. It was registered as part of the medical services in Mbabane that reached out to another sector of the population.

WHO
(World Health Organization in Geneva)

In his capacity as Minister of Health, Dr. Samuel was Swaziland's representative to the World Health Organization (WHO) and travelled often to meetings where representatives from many countries were present. WHO launched a plan and slogan of "Health for All by 2000." This enabled him to introduce and set in action Community Health Workers (*boNcucuteli*). These rural health promoters trained in basic first aid and home-based care and were sent out to visit homesteads in their residential areas. This program greatly helped mobilize child immunizations, alerted nurses in the primary health care centres to visit any serious care needs, and created a system to help relieve many of the health issues in the families around Swaziland, including nutrition, hygiene, and other safety conditions.

Dr. Samuel Hynd as Minister of Health representing Swaziland in Geneva, Switzerland, at the World Health Organization meetings, with Dr. Dlamini.

While in WHO, he served on the committee that researched the elimination of smallpox in the world. The committee's research led to the suspension, indefinitely, of the necessity for smallpox vaccinations worldwide.

As part of his WHO involvement, he was invited to Winnipeg, Canada, to present a research paper on one of his deep concerns for worldwide health. Because of the firsthand damage he had seen as a doctor that was directly related to substance abuse, Dr. Samuel had always taken a strong stand against it; in particular, tobacco smoking and the consumption of alcohol. He had seen too many cases of emphysema, lung cancer, oral cancer (mouth), strokes, and heart attacks caused by vascular problems related to tobacco and smoking. He had seen too many sick and inadequately nourished, premature babies due to insufficient nutrition from the placenta while in the womb because of the mother's smoking and alcohol use. He saw too many babies born in severe addiction and pain due to their mothers' substance abuse during pregnancy. He had also seen too many fights, stab wounds, and *knobkerrie*-damaged skulls showing up at the hospital in the middle of the night, on weekends, and especially on payday weekends due to people bingeing on alcohol. He had seen too many women coming in holding an ear to be sown back on because someone in a drunken rage had bitten it off. Worst of all were the Saturday night emergencies where innocent pedestrians or passengers and drivers in cars had been hit by drunken drivers. Deeper into the heart of the matter was the suffering of children growing up in these abusive and chaotic situations of substance abuse. Something needed to be done, but what could he do as Minister of Health to change the customs and behaviors of the Nation?

He addressed this in Cabinet with His Majesty the King and was able to pass legislation through Cabinet and Parliament that banned all alcoholic beverages from official government meetings, functions, and events in the Nation. Would that it had been banned from the entire Nation, but that is yet to come.

COSAD
(Council on Smoking, Alcohol and Drug Dependence)

As a member of the World Health Organization, Dr. Samuel presented a paper at the WHO conference in Winnipeg on smoking and alcohol and their devastation to the health and welfare of individuals and families and the cost to the Nation for the care and support of such substance abuse. He advocated the cessation of smoking in public and work places, thus eliminating the dangers of secondhand smoke to others. (Today, in many countries of the world, smoking is not allowed in public places.)

Following his presentation in Winnipeg, and after he learned the challenges and ravages other nations faced concerning alcohol, smoking, and drug abuse (in fact all substance abuse), he simply could not let the problems go on like this. So when he returned to Swaziland, he called a group together, and they talked about what to do. One member of the group was a chief matron (chief nursing officer), Mrs. Aileen Dlamini. She and Dr. Samuel invited a group of people to identify major individuals in the country who were also concerned about the problem.

"We can't just sit here and talk," Dr. Samuel said. "We need to address the problem and do battle."

COSAD: Council on Smoking Alcohol and Drug Dependence building in downtown Manzini. It served the whole country with education, prevention, counseling, advocacy, and legislation through Parliment.

The group formed an organization known as the Council on Smoking Alcohol and Drug Dependence (COSAD). Dr. Samuel spoke in schools, sugar mills, and at community events. There were parades held in cities and in stadiums throughout the country to raise awareness about the dangers of smoking and to discourage it.

Through COSAD, counselors were trained to help those who were trying to escape the snares of addiction. Swaziland did not establish a rehabilitation centre as clients were usually sent to South

Africa for treatment. It was only through the establishment of Teen Challenge by Kevin Ward, partnering with Teen Challenge UK, that people could receive help locally for addiction problems of smoking, alcohol, and drugs. To this day in Swaziland there is no public tobacco advertising. COSAD's work continued until 2013.

Leprosy Mission Board

Many years earlier when Dr. David Hynd was still practicing medicine in Swaziland, one of the major problems confronting the health of the Nation was leprosy. Those infected had to be removed from the communal lifestyle of the rural homesteads in order to prevent further contamination and infection. The British government built a beautiful place for lepers up in the mountains, but could not get anyone to run it. They came to talk with Dr. David about the situation. God had already prepared someone for the job.

Elizabeth Cole was a cowgirl riding her horse and herding cattle on the free range of Montana when God interrupted her life and called her to Swaziland as a missionary nurse to care for lepers. She immediately gave up her life on the open range and prepared herself by acquiring her nursing qualifications. She applied to come to Swaziland and informed Dr. David that she was coming to serve the lepers in the land. So when the government officials came to Dr. David in the 1940s asking if he could run the leper colony, he said "yes" because Elizabeth Cole was waiting in the wings and was ready to take over.

Elizabeth Cole was an amazing woman of God. She had an incredible hotline to Heaven. If Elizabeth prayed about anything, you had to get ready because God would bring it to pass. "I don't know any prayer she prayed that wasn't answered. You had to be careful on any matter she prayed about because God always answered her," said Dr. Samuel. Elizabeth Cole moved to the Leper Colony, as it was then called, and ran the small hospital for inpatients. She prepared one of the patients to be the pastor of the colony chapel located next to the hospital.

Mbuluzi Leprosy Mission in the mountains of the Hhlohho Region. Nestled on the ridge were the cottage hospital and the small church.

It was amazing that she was able to establish a working community for those lepers, to the point that they began to work the land. They planted and produced *mielies* (corn, the staple diet) and vegetables. They raised cows for milk and *emasi* (Swazi yogurt). This meant the leper colony was self-sustaining and the skills, self-respect, self-worth, and self-esteem of the lepers was enhanced, making for a happy and cheerful atmosphere in a very serious environment. It could have been so easy to focus on the missing limbs, gaping nostrils, and deformed faces where the ravages of the disease had taken its toll, but Elizabeth created a community of love, respect, and hope.

Elizabeth Cole, on one of her furlough trips, had traveled with Dr. David and Kanema Hynd through Europe and stopped at Oberammergau, Germany, to fulfill a dream they had all shared. They attended the Passion of Christ drama that the entire village community produces every ten years. When Elizabeth returned, she mobilized the entire family at the

Mbuluzi Leper Colony to produce the Christmas story as a pageant. They began with the annunciation of Gabriel to Mary on a hilltop overlooking the hospital and chapel. They then had a station where Joseph, asleep in his home, was visited by the angel to prepare him to take Mary as his betrothed. The whole community would then hobble down to "Bethlehem" and find no room at the "inn." (They used the little cottage hospital as the inn.) Then they would go to the *sibaya* (the cattle shed) to find Mary and Joseph there, and the latest little baby born in the community lying in the manger. Shepherds would come with their sheep and goats, and the wise men from the east would join in worship of the King of kings born in a lowly stable. What a humble reality was lived and acted out in their midst—the wonder of the love of God, even for those who had no limbs and those who were deformed and ugly by the world's standards. Samuel recalls, "Joining them each year for this pageant, after my mother and father retired to the leper colony for ten years, had to be one of the greatest highlights of our lives as a young family."

Elizabeth Cole was the most perfect and beautiful person to operate this colony. Later in her life, Queen Elizabeth II presented her with MBE (Honorable Member of British Empire) for her work among the lepers on Mbuluzi Mountain in Swaziland. She had a faithful, gentle, selfless love for mankind. Mary Bagley, another very special missionary nurse, all the way from Australia, followed Elizabeth Cole in this ministry to the rejected and the maimed leper community for many years.

After some time, leprosy was all but wiped out as a disease in Swaziland. Even though it was virtually gone, there had always been an International Leprosy Mission headquartered in Johannesburg. The purpose of this organization had been the eradication of leprosy. Dr. Samuel's function on this board had been to recognize the disease as a problem and to see that lepers received the medications they needed. Because of the success in eradicating and treating this disease, the question the committee faces today is: does the organization still need to exist? Just recently the board held its first meeting using Skype conferencing. What a drastic change from the early days of travel on horseback or by ox wagon!

Dr. Samuel and the rest of the committee worked to improve the living conditions of lepers and to see that they received necessary treatment. "When there were only six patients left in Swaziland at the leprosarium at Mbuluzi, we saw that we could bring them to the Manzini area to be treated. Depending on a patient's condition, he or she was either admitted to the RFM Hospital or treated as an outpatient," Dr. Samuel said. At the time of this writing, there are only two known cases of leprosy in Swaziland. A prefabricated office building is located at the ACTS II Clinic near Manzini with one retired nurse who monitors and manages the treatment and healing of those two patients.

The question then became what to do with the land where the Leprosy Colony had been located. The solution was an amazing idea that flourishes today.

ACAT
(African Cooperative Action Trust)

When the last of the lepers were moved out of the leprosarium, the responsibility for the land and buildings reverted to the government. The lepers had established farming procedures that had worked well, and all able-bodied lepers had worked the soil. Considering the fact that leprosy was being eradicated, a new use needed to be found for the colony.

Officials brought in the World Health Organization and the Food and Agricultural Organization (FAO) to decide how the place would now be used. The first idea was rehabilitation of the disabled. But FAO said, "We can't put people in wheelchairs here. It is very hilly, and their chairs would run away with them." As Minister of Health, Dr. Samuel waited until all ideas were discussed and exhausted. Then he presented the need for agricultural training and improved nutrition for

rural families. Most of the people of Swaziland were agricul-
turalists, each with one small holding for subsistence farming.
He had already started the African Cooperative Action Trust
(ACAT), and he now proposed a training centre for teaching
families improved, cooperative, agricultural methods and
strategies using Conservation Farming (popularly called
"Farming God's Way").

Dr. Samuel went to the Cabinet with the idea. ACAT's mission was to implement training and mentoring programs
aimed at equipping people to be sustainable in every aspect
of their lives and to influence, motivate, and assist others to
do the same. The idea was approved.

Ailene Dlamini, the Chief Nursing Officer who worked
alongside Dr. Samuel in the Ministry of Health, was retiring
from government at that time and was immediately recruited
to be the director of ACAT. She did a phenomenal job and was
the director for more than ten years, establishing the nation-
wide program, negotiating with families, communities, community leaders, and chiefs all over Swaziland. She celebrated
the tenth anniversary of ACAT at a trade fair in Manzini, along

Mbuluzi Leprosy Mission now used by ACAT for training courses and youth camps.

with thousands of other participants. The King renamed ACAT as "Lilima, Swaziland."

At the outset, some high school boys who were interested in the project had come to help. One of those boys, Enock Dlamini, later became the director of ACAT and has done a superb job. He has, in recent times, added the element of OVC (Orphans and Vulnerable Children) to the ACAT mix. One of the other boys, Danger Nhlabatsi, became the operations officer and has served superbly for the past twenty-three years with amazing success. He has just recently been recruited as the director of the Swaziland Red Cross.

The way the ACAT program works is unique. Attendees go to the Mbuluzi Training Centre farm for six weeks of training to learn how to increase their food output. Each family in Swaziland is assigned a small plot of ground by their chief—enough to sustain a family but not large enough to grow produce for profit. Under the ACAT plan, Dr. Samuel had two or three families join together their assigned plots of ground so they could grow enough produce for themselves and some to sell. The sale of produce enables families to manage their other needs such as clothing, building materials for their homes, furniture, school fees for their children, and other family commitments.

At the training centre, farmers are taught how to plant crops, alternating rows of corn and legumes—plants that take nitrogen from the soil with those that put it back. This is conservation planting. Dr. Samuel learned about this program in Natal. Families must come, agree to work together, and share what they are doing. They must allocate land they will work together, and they must establish a financial base by committing themselves to maintaining shared finances to procure a starter package. The starter package contains the specific inputs needed for the size of land that will make sufficient produce for the families, insuring they can purchase the input package the following year and for profits to be shared with the families involved as well as supplying their own nutritional needs. This has created further social and spiritual benefits of working together, being involved in one another's lives, and caring for one another's wellbeing.

This program is a good picture of Dr. Samuel's philosophy of caring for the body, soul, and spirit. For the body, ACAT provides healthier foods. For the soul, it provides nourishment through education programs that work. The spirit is fed because corporate daily devotions and a strong Christian emphasis are encouraged.

"ACAT is absolutely amazing," Dr. Samuel says. "It's a story in itself of God's provision for this little Nation."

In times of drought, ACAT projects have received the blessings of rain while other areas have remained dry. The whole ACAT idea was God's amazing timing of Dr. Samuel being in the right place at the right time. God placed Dr. Samuel in the Ministry of Health at the time the Leprosarium was no longer needed and at the time ACAT was ready to launch into a national program to improve nutrition, economic stability, and self-esteem in the agrarian communities. Independence brought Swaziland to a new place, and God placed His servant, Dr. Samuel Hynd, in a place where he could influence the national health through being Minister of Health.

SwaziMed

SwaziMed is the local health insurance program started by Dr. Samuel during his tenure as Minister of Health. Dr. Samuel was recently honored at the twenty-fifth anniversary celebration of the program.

There was a need for SwaziMed—dependable, affordable health care—because all of the money for health care insurance was going to South Africa. People were paying to join medical programs in South Africa. Local doctors in Swaziland could not establish practices because there was no insurance to pay them. If a patient saw a doctor in Swaziland, payment came through South Africa. Dr. Samuel got in touch with a medical aid person in South Africa who helped him establish a system in Swaziland that is working well now. At the time it started, only the large sugar estates had medical insurance. Now many companies use the SwaziMed program. Individual membership is still expensive. Many Swazis cannot afford it, so they still have no medical aid. That is most unfortunate.

Swazi Central Medical Supplies

While Minister of Health, Dr. Samuel also established the Swazi Central Medical Supply. There are no pharmaceutical manufacturing companies in Swaziland, and because the country is so small, it is not likely there ever will be. All medications are sourced externally. In the 1970s, hospitals, clinics, pharmacies, and even the government were getting drugs from many sources. Supplies were inconsistent as orders, deliveries, and storage were complicated. Sometimes there were meds and sometimes there were not. There were few drugs available for hospitals. Dr. Samuel set up big supply houses that stocked pharmaceutical supplies for the smaller stores and eliminated the problem of the shortage of supplies. Dr. Samuel didn't copy other countries' programs, as their programs didn't work well. He created his own, and what he created has served the country well.

CANGO
(Coordinating Assembly of Non-Governmental Organizations)

Early in his time as Minister of Health, Dr. Samuel was confronted with a perpetual problem that seemed to have no solution. The many wonderful non-governmental organizations, churches, and missions doing a significant work in the country needed to meet with the Minister of Health for many and varied issues. This created a problem, as time was always a factor. In 1978 he had an inspiration and established CANGO, the Coordinating Assembly of Non-Government Organizations. This meant that all the organizations wanting to help and that were trying to work with the government independently, could join and work together collectively. The association could choose representatives of the people from all of these non-governmental organizations to meet and figure out a way to work together. These organizations are the workhorses of charitable endeavors. CANGO currently leads the civil society in facilitating interventions such as the AIDS response and other community challenges, even to this day.

The Boys and Girls Brigade

This venture has proved to be a great blessing to Swaziland's young people. The Boys and Girls Brigade began in Scotland after World War II to help young people who found themselves adrift without mums and dads. Its function was to provide guidance, security, and confidence in dealing with the challenges in a nation recovering from the ravages of war. It was a Christian organization that ministered to the whole person with practical training in addition to spiritual training. It not only encouraged a devotional time, but also trained people in how to work together in a corporate endeavor. While Dr. Samuel was on furlough in the United Kingdom in the 1960s, he met leaders of this organization in Glasgow, Scotland, and immediately saw how it could benefit the youth in Swaziland.

To launch the program, Dr. Samuel called together some friends, with a heart for young people, and launched a chapter of the Boys and Girls Brigade in Hlatikhulu, where a Pastor of the Church of the Nazarene, Reverend Hadzebe, made a place available on his mission station for youngsters to meet after school and on weekends. He allocated a shed for them to begin their first enterprise project. Dr. Samuel bought fifty egg-laying chickens. The children were taught how to care for them. It was their responsibility to buy food for the chickens, collect their eggs, and sell them. The success of this Club led the way for others to set up hair salons, barber shops, and sewing projects.

The Brigade has its own marching band and was trained by the Brigadier Band Master of the National Correctional Services. He loved music and taught the kids how to play and how to care for their instruments. The instruments were donated through the International Boys and Girls Brigade in Australia. They also have a national camp at least once a year. This was another example of Dr. Samuel's philosophy of caring for the whole man. Scripture Union was active in schools and did a wonderful job of caring for the spiritual side of these young people. However, they didn't have the practical or entrepreneurial side. There was no organization similar to the Brigade.

Swaziland Conference of Churches

Dr. David's brainchild was to unite all the churches in Swaziland so that they would work together in prayer and support for the Kingdom of God in the Kingdom of Swaziland. He called the various denominations to come together (similar to something that had happened when the first missionaries came to Swaziland) to plan, strategize, and pray for God's guidance in how to serve the Kingdom of God in the Kingdom of Swaziland. Many years later, the World Council of Churches was established. Sadly, this led to a split between the denominational churches and the Swaziland Conference of Churches because of dissimilar views on the South African apartheid policy. The Catholics, Methodists, Anglicans, and Lutherans split off with the World Council of Churches while the other Churches remained within the Swaziland Conference of Churches.

Dr. Samuel brought World Relief into the country through the Swaziland Conference of Churches. The organization supported World Health for all. Part of the work of the Swaziland Conference of Churches was to help women who had no economic power get jobs. The Conference set up women's club meetings for handicrafts, income generation, skills development, Bible studies, and prayer under the leadership of

Matrine Lukhele, a former head teacher of the Evelyn Barring School in Nhlangano.

Dr. Samuel was Secretary to the Conference of Churches. Dr. David, after founding and acting as chairperson, remained as a member emeritus of the committee until his death. Later, Dr. Samuel served as treasurer and established an office using a prefabricated building. He purchased a desk, typewriter, filing cabinet, and other office equipment. Until then, there had been no central location for the organization. It had merely been a roaming committee with no employees. The new office building was located on the main street of Manzini.

Theodora Manana was the first employee and served as receptionist, secretary, and bookkeeper. After this reorganization, the Swaziland Conference of Churches took on the huge project of establishing the work of the Swaziland Conference of Churches to spread the Good News of Jesus Christ and to raise up disciples who knew and understood the Word and ways of God. First, the Conference purchased two plots of land on the main street of Manzini between Nkhosenhlaza and Ngwane Street. The first plot of land was a mango orchard. The second plot had a government house on it that became the office. Some of the rooms were rented out. The rent helped support the fledgling organization. One office was rented to the International Tabernacle, a church that was just being started by Reverend Absalom Dlamini in the George Hotel, located across the street. He was a former principal and lecturer of New Haven Bible College, an Evangelical College in the south of Swaziland. He later became a Cabinet Minister serving several portfolios including the third highest position in the land as Minister of Economic Planning and Development.

SBIS
(Swaziland Broadcast Information Services)

Christian Radio in Swaziland was born in Dr. David's living room with a reel-to-reel tape recorder. Miss Joan Scutt, missionary of the South Africa General Mission, would travel and collect sermons from various pastors at regional or public meetings. These were recorded and broadcast by Christian Radio. Later on at the time of independence, the government took over the equipment of Christian Broadcasting, agreeing forever that Christian programming would be central to its overall programming. The broadcasting system has now become Swaziland Broadcast Information Services (SBIS), and it has many programs that are run by Christian Media Centre.

Christian Media Centre

Dr. Samuel attended both the Billy Graham International Conference in Lausanne, Switzerland, and Lausanne II, a second Billy Graham conference held in the Philippines. There he was challenged to take the Gospel to the airwaves. So, of course, that is what he did.

The Christian Media Centre was the dream of Dr. Samuel as a means of extending the ministry of the body of Christ through the media of radio waves, television, and the production of sound and video presentations, messages, and programs. He was able to contact a large number of Christian organizations who together raised the funds for a two-story building to occupy the first plot purchased by the Swaziland Conference of Churches. Dr. Samuel borrowed money from the Christian Holland Media Agency to help out.

A man named Karl Smensguarde helped with the Christian Media building. Smensguarde of the Swedish Mission had been the chairperson of the Swedish Free Missionary work in Swaziland. A young missionary, Alex van der Merwe, from Pretoria, South Africa, came to set up the studio with cameras, lights, and soundproofing.

The facility housed a large recording and video studio that had been soundproofed and fitted with lights, cameras, and other video effects and some stage props. It also had two audio sound rooms for recording programs that would be aired on the radio. In order to establish a solid financial base, the Christian Media Centre was constructed with apartments or flats on the upper floor that could be rented out. On the ground floor was a space for a large Christian bookstore, which was run by the Christian Literature Centre of the United Kingdom. Also located on a second property there were three single-story apartments also to sustain the Swaziland Conference of Churches.

Christian Media Centre in Manzini houses audio and video studios, the Swaziland Conference of Church Head Offices, and the Christian Literature Centre bookstore.

His Majesty King Mswati III came and opened the Media Centre, giving His blessing and endorsement. The King immediately recruited the president of the Swaziland Conference of Churches, Rev. Nicholas Nyawo, after he heard his speech that day. Nyawo became the president of the King's trust foundation called *Tibio TakaNgwane*. He was further entrusted by the King to establish an umbrella body for all the Christian Churches in Swaziland bringing the three strands together: the Swaziland Conference of Churches, the Council of Swaziland Churches and the League of Swaziland Churches.

The facility Dr. Samuel opened has served as the head offices for the Swaziland Conference of Churches, and the Christian Media Centre has produced programs for Swazi TV and other programs promoting the Gospel far and wide. Also, the radio programs have been used on Swaziland National Broadcasting, as well as, the Trans World Radio.

Manzini Town Council Chaplain

One of Dr. Samuel's first engagements, beyond the medical and church work at the Mission Station on the hill above Bremersdorp/Manzini, was to birth a vision he had for a citywide celebration of the resurrection of our Lord Jesus on Easter Sunday. He was granted permission to hold an early morning service that would begin before the sun rose on a hill that was the highest point above the town overlooking Manzini. It was next to the tower that supplied the town with water. Each year on Easter Sunday morning, crowds ascend the hill on foot, in vans, in *bakkis*, and in minibuses during the predawn chill and darkness.

The program included songs of praise and rejoicing, prayers of thanksgiving, and the reading of the Word of God, telling the story of when first the women, then Peter and John, ran to the tomb to find it empty. The crowd on Manzini's hill rejoices at daybreak for "He is risen!"

Years later when the Manzini Town Council was officially formed by elections, Dr. Samuel was nominated and elected as town chaplain. This meant he opened every council meeting with prayer and a brief devotional from the Word of God. These meetings were usually held in the evenings on Tuesdays, as most of the members were fully engaged in farming, banking, or commerce during the day. He continued in this role for more than thirty years until the town council was restructured to have a fully employed staff and an elected mayor.

It was in his role as town chaplain that he invited Michael Cassidy and the Africa Enterprise Ministries to come for a "Manzini for Jesus" campaign. This venture involved weeks of preparation, training counselors, and preparing churches for the influx of new believers who would be born again during the weeklong campaign. Banners and posters covered every wall and tree in the downtown area and surrounding communities. Announcements were made on radio, TV, and by vans with speakers on top that would drive up and down the roads calling people to come. The campaign was a huge success. Thousands of people were born again and brought into all the various churches and denominations for baptism and discipleship. It was a new day for Manzini!

Manzini City Council where Rev. Dr. Samuel Hynd served as town chaplain.

This was followed in 1992 by the one hundred year anniversary celebration of the city of Manzini. A Centenary Thanksgiving Service was held on Sunday, 4 October 1992, at the International Trade Fair Arena. As Chaplain, Dr. Samuel brought a historical message to thousands of excited citizens of the city. He used 2 Chronicles 7:12-16 (NKJV) as his theme.

I have heard your prayer, and have chosen this place for Myself as a house of sacrifice. When I shut up heaven and there is no rain, or command the locusts to devour the land, or send pestilence among My people, if My people who are called by My name will humble themselves, and pray and seek My face, and turn from their wicked ways, then I will hear from heaven, and will forgive their sin and heal their land. Now My eyes will be open and My ears attentive to prayer made in this place. For now I have chosen and sanctified this house, that My name may be there forever; and My eyes and My heart will be there perpetually.

He briefly summarized Manzini's humble beginnings—how in 1885, Mr. Bremer and Mr. Wallestein established a small store and hotel by the river (now known as the Mzimnene River) on land contributed by Chief Manzini Motsa. Then he talked about the confusion of bounty-seeking foreigners looking for land concessions for farming, grazing, and mineral scouting. He summarized that just as Israel had faced challenges, so Manzini, as a community, had faced challenges, especially when King Bhunu (King of Swaziland from 1895-1899) was accused of murdering Mbhabha Nsibandze (Royal Governor) and his collaborators. The King was found guilty in a trial held under the trees just above the present day City Council buildings and was fined.

It was an unsettled time in the country and white settlers became afraid that the Swazi Impis (Swazi regiments of warriors serving the King) would attack them, so they dug trenches on the hillside overlooking the town to stand their ground and protect their families. Trenches could still be found when Dr. Samuel was a boy. He once found one in an area now known as the Trelawney Park suburb.

Dr. Samuel likened the city of Manzini in 1992 to Jerusalem when King Solomon had built a new temple. In Manzini this temple was not of stones from the earth but rather of living stones. These living stones were the people of God who were called by His name and who put their trust in Him. In the same way that Joshua called the people of Israel into a covenant, Dr. Samuel called Manzini into a covenant: "And the people said to Joshua, 'The LORD our God we will serve, and His voice we will obey!' . . . 'This stone shall be a witness to us, for it has heard all the words of the LORD which He spoke to us'" (Joshua 24:24, 27 NKJV).

Dr. Samuel had a wooden cross made from a tree from the Bhunya Forest, which was located in the northern mountains of Swaziland. He also got a huge, special stone from the Embhekelweni Royal Residence (where King Bhunu had resided) and set it up in the arena as a testament and sign of the commitment made: "To serve the Lord God Jehovah and to love our neighbors as ourselves." This Manzini Covenant was made on Sunday, 4 October 1992.

Sharpe Memorial Church
Board Membership

Shortly after Dr. Samuel had arrived in Swaziland with his young wife Rosemarie, the members of the growing Sharpe Memorial Church of the Nazarene, located on the main road coming into the city, nominated and elected him to serve on the church board. This meant that he was as fully part of church life in Swaziland as he had been as a student in Glasgow, Scotland. In spite of his many responsibilities in the hospital and clinics, he kept his weekly commitment to participate in a day of fasting with the men's fellowship of the church on Thursdays and to meet for the one-hour prayer service on Thursday nights in the Old Stone Church, just as Rosemarie met with the women's fellowship in the Old Stone Church on Wednesday afternoons for prayer. He served faithfully on the church board for nearly sixty years and was nominated annually from the early 1950s until 2012. He still serves today as an elder in the church and faithfully attends Sunday services, camp meetings, and other revival services held throughout the year. His service to the church is one of the loves of his life, as the church not only serves the

Manzini community, but also all of the boarding students in the Manzini Nazarene High School, the Nazarene College of Nursing, and the Nazarene College of Education.

Southern African Nazarene University

For many years Dr. Samuel realized the Swazi people needed more education than they were getting. He dreamed of the country having a university. "I didn't think I would live to see my dream of a university fulfilled," says Dr. Samuel.

In the 1990s, the International Church of the Nazarene redefined Swaziland as a full member of the denomination, rather than as a mission work. This meant that the National Board of Swaziland was now responsible for the development of all the ministries of the Church of the Nazarene in Swaziland: its hospital, clinics, schools, training centres, colleges, and churches. At that time, the National Board (this is a board of elected church leaders called "superintendents" that are similar to bishops in other denominations) asked Dr. Samuel to be the chairperson of the Swaziland Nazarene Health Institution, which included the hospitals, clinics, and the Nurses Training College. The organization would operate under the National Board (made up of preachers).

Then in 1993 there was a big shift. Because Swaziland was no longer designated as a mission, all Nazarene missionary personnel were relocated to missions elsewhere in the world. Dr. Samuel had not been a part of the Nazarene leadership since he had left his missionary service to serve the Kingdom as a Cabinet member. Now, out of a clear blue sky he was called to be the chairperson of health and medical work for the Swaziland Nazarene Health Institute. This included the hospital, clinics, and college of nursing. From that position he went to His Majesty with a strategic development plan, which included the establishment of a university.

It was during this time that Dr. Samuel and his board appointed a young PhD graduate in Nursing Administration from Manchester University as principal of the College of Nursing, Dr. Winnie Nhlengethwa. She is a woman of amazing leadership qualities. (At the writing of this book, she has been appointed as vice-chancellor of the Southern African Nazarene University.)

Dr. Samuel influenced a young man, the chairman of the National Board, Rev. Simeon Mahlalela, who established a steering committee with the task of setting up a university. This young man nominated Dr. Samuel to the committee, and thereby began the process of Dr. Samuel seeing his dream of a Nazarene University come true.

While Dr. Samuel was chairman of the board, the board worked together with the Japanese to build the great hall and the library of the Nursing School. Dr. Winnie Nhlengethwa was able to raise funds and support to build a state-of-the-art

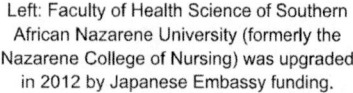

Left: Faculty of Health Science of Southern African Nazarene University (formerly the Nazarene College of Nursing) was upgraded in 2012 by Japanese Embassy funding.

Right: Faculty of Education of Southern African Nazarene University, formerly the Nazarene Teacher Training College.

Left: Southern African Nazarene University building housing the Vice Chancellor's office and other administrative services.

Faculty of Health Sciences. It is a three-story building that stands high above the Jacaranda and Flamboyant trees growing around the original twenty-five-acre farm where the first stone house and the Stone Church were built.

Colleges in the United States and in the United Kingdom helped bring the vision into being. The vision was to amalgamate the three existing tertiary institutions of the Church of the Nazarene into what was the Higher Education Commission, including the Nazarene Theological College at Siteki.

When, at long last, the registrations, regulations, standards of performance, and curricula inspections were completed, Dr. Samuel spoke at the school's inauguration. "This is my dream come true," he told the crowd that was seated in the Nursing College Lecture Theatre, a look of wonder in his eyes at all that had been accomplished.

Today, hundreds of students are learning how to build a better Swaziland at the fully registered and internationally recognized Southern African Nazarene University with degrees and diplomas. It will shortly be bringing on board other faculties and course programs such as Social Welfare Degrees and specialized programs to incorporate handicapped students.

National Coroner

Part of Dr. Samuel's duties throughout his years as a medical doctor and superintendent of the RFM Hospital and Minister of Health was to do postmortem examinations and then to testify in court as to the cause of death. Some of his challenging cases involved those who were victims of baptisms by some Christian sects. These deceased converts had often been epileptics who had died as a result of being plunged into cold water and held down too long, initiating a seizure. Dr. Samuel didn't like his job as national coroner. "I'd spend the whole day healing people, and then in the evenings, I had to go examine dead people in the mortuary. I never enjoyed this part of the job," he said.

UMCULU Bible Trek

1994 marked the 150th anniversary of the Holy Bible's coming to Swaziland. By way of review, remember that the Swazi regiment had been sent by His Majesty King Somhlolo to bring the *Umculu*—the Word of God—to Swaziland. The Swazi regiment then accompanied the assigned Methodist missionary, Reverend Alison and two Basutu evangelists from Thaba 'Nchu to Swaziland entering through the southern border. When the evangelists had arrived at Embangweni, the Royal Residence, the King allocated a mountain at Mahamba for their home and centre. From that time forward, the Methodist Mission was established. Today, the historic Stone Church and also the new large church built in 1997 are located at the foot of the mountain. The mountain has been and still is the home of the pastors, a clinic, and a school as well as a large auditorium for church services.

Mahamba Methodist Church built in the 1800s was the first Christian Church in Swaziland.

To commemorate the coming of the Word of God to Swaziland, the Somhlolo Festival of Praise committee presented a paper to the Cabinet, asking for a seven-week national celebration. A wooden ark was built and was painted gold as a replica of the Ark of the Covenant that Israel carried throughout its early history. The original Ark of the Covenant contained the Torah, manna, and Aaron's rod that budded. In Swaziland's case, the Ark of the Covenant replica contained the first printing of a brown leather-bound copy of the SiSwati Bible (*LiBhayibheli LeliNgcwele*) printed by the Bible Society of South Africa. The replica Ark and Bible were carried on foot from town to town all around Swaziland.

A reenactment of the *Umculu* Bible Trek began at the border gate of Swaziland, at Mahamba, with four Methodist men arriving in traditional attire after having travelled to Thaba' Nchu and back remembering the warriors who travelled with Reverend Allison. These men were met by the Prime Minister and the full Cabinet of the Kingdom of Swaziland: members of Parliament, church leaders of the country, and the King's representatives. They marched from the border on foot, holding banners. They were accompanied to the original Mahamba Church (which had just been renovated) by the Royal Swaziland Police brass band. There at the church, a service of thanksgiving launched the *Umculu* Bible Trek.

Young people from all over Swaziland gave themselves voluntarily for seven weeks to travel with the Bible, doing dramas and presenting the Gospel in the highways and byways and in the communities located in the hills and valleys of the Kingdom of Swaziland. At each community, the pastors from the town would come together and carry the "Ark of the Covenant," which contained the Word of God, on their shoulders. As soon as they reached a community or town, a rally would be held in the marketplace or a football stadium. Services were held in the evenings in each place where the team stopped for the night. Thousands upon thousands of people chose to believe in the God, who had troubled Himself enough to leave His throne in glory and come and talk to the founding King of the Nation about the wondrous story of the Son of God. This story is about Jesus, who left His glory to come, live, and die on earth. He did this to show us the way to God and to win us positions as sons and daughters of God. In some places, drama was used to convey the powerful love of God that surpasses the power of any witchcraft or devilish powers.

The media—both radio and television— followed the *Umculu* Bible Trek from place to place. This was truly a high-profile, triple-jubilee celebration. It culminated at the National Somhlolo Stadium on 22 July, bringing together the national public holiday celebration of the Somhlolo Festival of Praise, and the thanksgiving of the Nation for the coming of the Gospel of Christ. King Mswati III was presented with a leather-bound, complete translation of the first SiSwati Bible. This was the end of a twenty-seven-year project of the South African Bible Society and the Swaziland Bible Society. Dr. Samuel remembers the translation of the Swazi Bible as one of the highlights of his lifetime. It was his joy to have had the opportunity to be part of the implementation of such a marvelous, national commemoration of God's work in the Kingdom of Swaziland for the establishment of the Kingdom of God.

Torch Runs

Torch runs began internationally. The call was for every nation to participate. Dr. Samuel and the Somhlolo Festival of Praise committee headed up the team that would organize the *torch* to be carried through Swaziland from the southern border to the northern border. It would stop along the way for rallies and celebrations of revival. These celebrations were for the Good News and the Light that had come into the world through Jesus and had ignited the people's hearts.

This first torch run was part of the worldwide run. In Africa, the flame was lit in Cape Town, the mother city, and then was carried on foot from town to town and city to city. It travelled up the east coast and into Swaziland at the Lavumisa border in the south, through the centre of the country, stopping in Big Bend, Siphofaneni, Manzini, Lobamba, and Mbabane for rallies and celebrations of praise and evangelistic invitations to the saving grace of God. The flame then passed through Ngwenya, one of the northern border posts, and into South Africa as it continued up through the continent of Africa from Swaziland.

The next year, each nation was encouraged to have a national torch run. Dr. Samuel desperately wanted Swaziland to be a part of it, so he called his daughter, Elizabeth, to come from Japan to organize and mobilize the Round Swaziland Torch Run for the Swaziland Conference of Churches. Churches, ministries, schools, and colleges were all involved from the north, south, east, and west. No place was left out, and no place was overlooked.

After the flame was ignited, it was carried by young people from community to community where they held rallies. The Round Swaziland Torch Run ended at the Royal Residence of Ludzidzini with a rally attended by Their Majesties, King Mswati III and the Queen Mother, the *Indlovulkazi*. It was at this rally, while a lady evangelist preached, that His Majesty stood up publically to acknowledge the saving grace of Jesus Christ and to testify by raising His hand that He chose Jesus to rule and reign in His heart. As the Swazi's say *"Ngiyamu Ketsu Jesu!"* Thousands were born into the Kingdom of God during those six weeks of rallies and services in communities all around Swaziland.

Somhlolo Festival of Praise

King Somhlolo's historic vision is an integral part of the national history, health, prosperity, peace, and celebration of Swaziland. This event in history had been kept alive through tradition and by word-of-mouth stories, but not through any formal recognition. Dr. Samuel Hynd, Norman Malinga, and Douglas Litchfield became inspired to bring legitimacy to God's divine intervention in the life of the Nation. The Somhlolo Festival of Praise was born—the national celebration of the coming of the Gospel to Swaziland. The Festival is held on 22 July each year.

Before Dr. Samuel organized the Somhlolo Festival, the SADAC regional meeting had been chaired by King Mswati III and had been hosted in Swaziland in 1989. Part of the program of events for these meetings had included a festival held in the national stadium. It had consisted of a terrible music festival with openly practiced sex. It was extremely vulgar. Everyone, including the Royalty, was horrified by this jazz festival. Dr. Samuel went to see the elders at the Lobamba offices of the King to report that this event was a horrendous disgrace and not in keeping with Swazi ways. The Queen Mother suggested he overcome the effects of this jazz festival with a Celebration of Praise.

Norman Malinga, Dr. Samuel's long-time friend, had been the Ambassador for Swaziland at the United Nations. Dr. Samuel told Malinga that he had gone to the Royal Elders and the King's office about this festival situation. Dr. Samuel shared the Queen's suggestion with him. They formed a committee of business people: a banker, Andy McGuire, Dr. Busa Xaba, Norman Malinga, Douglas Litchfield, Dr. Samuel Hynd, and Mike Boast of Sugar Estates. Norman shared his dream for an International Prayer Breakfast as had been done in the United Nations annually.

As Cabinet Minister, Dr. Samuel was able to write and prepare a Cabinet paper to secure the formal use of this public holiday for the celebration and thanksgiving of the Word of God. The paper requested not only the Royal Swazi Convention Centre be reserved as the place to hold the International Prayer Breakfast annually on 22 July but also the National Stadium for the Somhlolo Festival of Praise. When this paper passed the Cabinet and was presented to His Majesty, He not only approved the idea, but was so thrilled that He called for a Thanksgiving Service to be held at the National Stadium on the Sunday nearest to 22 July, which would bring all Christians together to give thanks for the goodness of God in the land.

The purpose of the Somhlolo Festival of Praise was to keep alive the divine heritage of the Nation through praise and thanksgiving. The first International Prayer Breakfast, Song and Music Festival, and Sunday Thanksgiving Service began in July of 1991. This developed into a four-day, national event. The Public Holiday on 22 July was the day of the International Prayer Breakfast, followed by a pastors' conference in the day-time and all day prayer in the National Church at Lobamba. One year, the Song and Music festival was held with choirs, which included a Welsh Male Voice Choir from the United Kingdom, praise teams, and professional Gospel musicians and artists from all over the South African Region (Liz Pass, Derek Nzibandze, and Deborah were among them). The Sun-day Thanksgiving Service in the stadium was graced by His Majesty, King Mswati III and Her Majesty, the Queen Mother, the *Indlovukati*, as well as diplomats, the Prime Minister, mem-bers of Cabinet and of Parliament, church leaders, and inter-national guests and speakers. A youth dimension was part and parcel of these events. Operation Mobilization, Youth for Christ, and Youth With A Mission were invited to send teams

King Mswati III graces the Festival of Praise at the Somholo National Stadium at Lobamba.

into the country for the whole month preceding the national weekend's events. They visited and ministered in schools and churches and held rallies in the marketplaces. Throughout the country, in the evenings and on the weekends during the month of July and culminating in the Sunday thanksgiving service, they held youth rallies that were broadcast live, both on SBIS and Swazi TV, the national carrier. During each of the four nights of evening services, crowds filled the Lobamba National Church and the events were aired live nationally on SBIS, so no one was left out of the events.

When Meshack Shongwe was the Principal Secretary of Home Affairs, the Cabinet passed a paper making this day an official part of the national calendar. His Majesty saves the day each year to be in the Nation and to participate in the worship and preaching of the Word of God. He usually sends one of his brothers to speak on his behalf at the International Prayer Breakfast on the national public holiday of 22 July, but Their Majesties personally attend the Thanksgiving Service held in the National Somhlolo Stadium. Each brings an exhortation and word from the Lord. His Majesty's messages are lively, life-giving messages of hope, and His central theme is always that this Word of God made flesh in Jesus Christ of Nazareth must live inside the heart of every person in Swaziland.

When the Somhlolo Festival of Praise was launched, the International Prayer Breakfast at the Royal Swazi Convention Centre was launched as well. The first breakfast was held on the day after the Preferential Trade Area (PTA) was hosted in Swaziland in 1989. This Annual Summit of the Presidents of East, Central, and Southern African countries was held at the Royal Swazi Convention Centre. Since all the heads of state, dignitaries, diplomats, heads of businesses, and heads of churches came to the PTA summit they were also able to attend the Prayer Breakfast on the last day before all of them returned to their home states. His Majesty and the elders agreed, and so began a tradition that has continued annually—an International Prayer Breakfast and the Somhlolo Festival of Praise.

At the first Prayer Breakfast, Michael Cassidy, president and founder of Africa Enterprise and President Kaunda of Kenya, the international representative, were keynote speakers. The annual breakfast has featured international speakers such as Angus Buchan of Shalom Ministries in KwaZulu, Natal; Mikizwe Makhanya of Zimbabwe; Bishop Wale Oke of Nigeria; Samuel Doktorian of Lebanon; June McKinney of End-Time Harvest USA; Langton Gatsi of the All Africa House of Prayer, Zimbabwe; Janine Maxwell of Heart for Africa USA; Bishop Muhinde of Uganda; and John Mulinde of Africa Enterprise.

The Somhlolo Festival of Praise also organized Swaziland's participation in the global "March for Jesus" movement. This began in London in 1987, emerging from the friendship of three church groups: Pioneer, led by Gerald Coates; Ichthus, led by Roger Foster; and Youth With A Mission, led by Lynn Green together with worship leader, Graham Kendricks. In the next three years, it spread all over the United Kingdom, Europe, and North America. In the First Global March for Jesus on Pentecost Saturday 1994, Swaziland was part of 170 nations that participated worldwide, involving over ten million Christians and covering all the time zones on the earth. This worldwide movement called each city and country to participate annually in May or June at the celebration of the Pentecost—the coming of the Holy Spirit in outpouring power. First, it was held in the two major cities of Swaziland—Mbabane and Manzini—and then, in its final year on 10 June 2000, it was held in ninety-four towns, villages, and cities in Swaziland, using banners, public speakers, and marching bands through the streets, recruiting everyone to join in declaring Jesus as King of kings and Lord of all.

In 1997, following the Global Consultation on World Evangelism (GCOWE) held in Pretoria, South Africa, which had emerged from the Billy Graham Lausanne I and II Conferences, the Somhlolo Festival of Praise added a dimension of national prayer, intercession, and a focus on children. The first

National Children's Camp, held in a tent near the National Church, was a small beginning. Unfortunately, the weather was dismally cold and dreary with torrential rains. Each year the Children's Camp grew, bringing 300, 600, and 1,200 children to the National Church for the weekend. These camps focused on developing the children's understanding of the power of the Word of God and of praise and worship in their lives and the life of the Nation. Soon the numbers began to be overwhelming, and the focus shifted to inviting schools to send the leaders in each grade to attend these camps. In 2006, another shift in focus was made as it was found that orphans and vulnerable children were struggling with behavioral, emotional, and academic problems. The camps then took on the challenge of working with the children through their loss and grief issues, helping them develop resilience.

In 1998, another dimension was added to the Festival of Praise when a Pastors' Conference was held on the Saturday prior to the Thanksgiving Service, bringing pastors of all different denominations and congregations together to be encouraged and fed on the Word of God. In 1999, a women's dimension was added with the theme of "Arise and Shine in '99." Women's conferences were held in fourteen cities throughout Swaziland.

In the year 2000, the Festival of Praise went national and had a four-day "rolling" conference in sixteen city centres throughout the country. This meant that on the first day of the celebration it would begin in one city centre, and while that celebration went on for four days, the next celebration would begin in another city on the second day and would also go on for four days. The same thing would happen on the third and fourth day, as the festival moved on to the third and fourth city centres. At any one time, at least four cities somewhere in the country were celebrating. The celebration took place in fourteen city centres throughout the country. The celebrations culminated in July at the Somhlolo National Stadium with the Sunday Thanksgiving Service.

Each day of the celebration had a different focus. The first day was the Children's Festival with a "March for Jesus," as school bands and cheerleaders led people in praise through the streets. This was followed by a children's rally. The second day focused on praise and worship seminars for pastors, church leaders, and anyone who wanted to participate. It was led by a Jewish Messianic dance and worship team with a Youth Rally in the evening. This was followed on the third day with a full day of prayer and intercession. Finally, on the fourth day, a "mini-festival" was held, presenting the saving grace of God and the wonderful work of salvation through the death and resurrection of Jesus Christ of Nazareth.

In the following year, mini-festivals were launched in fourteen to sixteen communities around the country because people wanted the speakers, the celebration, the Word, the praise, and the thanksgiving to become a part of their local communities, as travel to the Lobamba area was expensive and limited the number of people who could be involved. Thus, local committees of pastors and church leaders arranged for local mini-festivals to be held during the week of 22 July, each year.

Partnering with Africa Enterprise, the Somhlolo Festival of Praise Committee organized Operation Sunrise, which focused on fifty major cities throughout Africa for fifty days of outreach and evangelism in 2002. Mbabane and Manzini were both target cities.

In June of 2006, the Global Billy Graham Crusade swept the world with the message of salvation. This was an amazing feat of technology and love. The Somhlolo Festival of Praise Committee embraced the task of bringing Swaziland into this ministry. Sixteen pastors were selected to join others in Midrand, near Johannesburg, for training sessions. They were to learn how a crusade that was being held live in Argentina could be transformed so that it was able to reach the entire world.

Dr. Samuel was the chairperson, at that time, and led the team in a great learning curve. The Christian Media Centre's missionary technician, Alex van der Merwe, was a tremendous blessing as he had much of the technical knowledge. The pastors were called together for a national meeting to introduce the concept of a global, week-long crusade that would take place live in Buenos Aires, would be transmitted by satellite around the world, downloaded in Mbabane, and recorded on video tapes. Then the video tapes would be delivered by car to the participating centres. The translators at these locations would practice translating the video into SiSwati so that it fit into the same timeframe that the Spanish translator used as he translated Billy Graham's English message into Spanish, line by line.

The pastors, fraternities, and interdenominational church leadership committees that were willing to take on the project returned home to discuss with their churches and leadership the opportunity of having a Billy Graham Crusade that would be held simultaneously with others all over the world. Sixteen venues came on board and committed themselves. All the churches in those communities registered for counselor training so that they would be able to lead seekers to an experience of receiving salvation. The interpreters had to be trained to effectively translate in the specific amount of time that they had. The technicians had to be trained to set up projectors, screens, and video machines with loudspeakers. Churches had to be prepared for the discipleship and care of the newborn Christians who would be added to the Body of Christ. Ushers had to be trained to handle the crowds and the ministry time at the close of each service.

God was good, the weather was good, and roads were drivable so the video tapes could be delivered daily. Electric power was stable as there were no storms, and the weather was comfortable, so people came out by the thousands each night. However, none of the venues were adequate for the crowds. Sheets were hung up in the city streets to use as screens where the messages could be projected. In some places, the team would use the outside walls of a city hall or of the largest church in town. The whole country was abuzz with the global outreach of the love of God through the heart and ministry of one man, Billy Graham from North Carolina, and his faithful team and supporters. Swaziland would never be the same after this major proclamation of the saving grace of God through the life, death, and resurrection of His Son.

When the Somhlolo Festival celebrated its twenty-first-anniversary year in 2012, new elements were added and a restructuring took place. The International Prayer Breakfast became a National Prayer Breakfast with a new location, as there were too many attendees for the Royal Swazi Convention Centre to handle. The Friday prior to the Festival was reserved for a National Symposium. This was a day for academic papers and research to be presented with regard to the historical, prophetic, political, spiritual, and social impact of the vision of King Somhlolo. The children's camps were replaced by a National Children's Day at the Somhlolo National Stadium. Children by the hundreds were bused in from all the regions of Swaziland as part of the event.

Today, 22 July is still a national, public holiday and has become the day to celebrate the coming of the Word of God—the very life of Christ—to the Nation. The date is amazing. Annually, on the twenty-second day of the seventh month, Israel celebrates a public holiday called Simchat Torah—the celebration of the Word of God—when families dance in the streets, joyfully celebrating the Word of God. The men, in some cases, carry the scrolls of the Torah. In other cases, they carry their firstborn son—the type and symbol of the Christ child, God's first and only begotten Son. It is Dr. Samuel's joy and privilege to have been part of establishing this celebration to honor the Word of God and the grace of God, as He brought eternal light, life, and hope into this tiny mountain Kingdom.

Cheshire Homes

God's heart in Dr. Samuel has always been for the marginalized and suffering people. It was Dr. Samuel's privilege to be used by God to introduce and establish Cheshire Homes in

Swaziland, to ensure the care of handicapped individuals in the Nation. The Homes recently celebrated their twenty-fifth anniversary of service in Swaziland. Today, stroke victims, accident victims, and the like, all come to Cheshire Homes for help with physical therapy, occupational therapy, and other services including HIV testing.

Upgrading RFM Hospital

Raleigh Fitkin Memorial Hospital has always been well used. Not only has it been a hospital, but also a teaching centre where students can do their practical training. In time, even the renovated buildings of the 1960s began to go downhill and desperately needed remodeling and refurbishing. Dr. Gary Morsch, a former medical student who had come for his student practical training at RFM hospital in the time when Dr. Samuel was still medical superintendent, came for a visit in his capacity as president and founder of Heart to Heart, a medical emergency mission charity. Dr. Gary wanted to spend some time with his former mentor and colleague, Dr. Samuel. During that time, Dr. Samuel shared with Dr. Gary the heartache he felt about the condition of the hospital. The two doctors and Barbi Moore, Heart to Heart's administrative assistant, toured the hospital together, and when they saw its condition, they were utterly distressed. They decided to do something about it. They returned to the United States where Barbi shared their distress with her pastor, Reverend David Busic of Bethany First Church in Bethany, Oklahoma, near Oklahoma City.

This Church had a long relationship with Swaziland as it was the home church of that early missionary of long ago, Harmon Schelzenbach. Pastor Busic prepared a team of church leadership to visit Swaziland and see the situation for themselves. From this visit, an organization called "Swaziland Partnership"—a partnership between Bethany First Church and the Church of the Nazarene in Swaziland—was formed. Barbi resigned her position at Heart to Heart and became fully employed as administrator of the Swaziland Partnership with Reverend David Busic, where they worked to restore RFM Hospital, to do medical work in the clinics and health centres in the country, and to accomplish other church-related projects of the Church of the Nazarene in Swaziland

The Swaziland Partnership worked with Dr. Gary Morsch and many others to raise funds and awareness of the need. Barbi Moore arranged for Gospel Outreach (GO) teams to come and serve in Swaziland. These GO teams were made up of volunteers with the skills or the expertise needed to bring about a change, primarily in the hospital, and then in other areas of ministry by improving the physical facility and morale and bringing training for various areas of need. The GO teams even set up a fully-equipped dental clinic at RFM Hospital.

Left: RFM Hospital 2011. The rehabilitation of the Hospital boosted morale and quality of service delivery as well as renewed national and international support. Official opening of the new outpatient unit at RFM Hospital was by His Majesty King Mswati III.

Right: 2013 medical services continue to be enhanced and are a far cry from the days of Samuel riding with his father on horseback to visit the nearby homesteads. Now emergency services with trained paramedics serve the centre of the country with a much needed state-of-the-art ICU. The ICU was donated by the Republic of China in Taiwan.

Left: Current view of Outpatient Department of RFM Hospital (2013).

The result has been that the RFM Hospital has been awarded the "Best Practice Medical Facility" in Southern Africa and is once again the place of relief and healing for hundreds and hundreds of those in need of help for body, soul, and spirit.

*   *   *

During these years of service, Dr. Samuel's life was rich with purpose and meaning. There were clinics to open, primary health care centres to build and establish throughout the country, Hlatikulu Hospital in the Shiselweni region to renovate, and speeches to give throughout the country that would enable him to raise awareness of the need for healthy nutrition and lifestyles for the total man. It was during this time that alcohol was banned from all official functions held by the government, ensuring safe and appropriate behavior at such functions.

After Dr. Samuel's term as Minister of Health, he and Phyllis (before her untimely illness and death) took an extended vacation and visited Elizabeth and Margie in Hong Kong. They celebrated Christmas dinner with friends in a luxury apartment in Repulse Bay on the south side of Victoria Island, which still had much of the British flavor of life. They attended the midnight Christmas Eucharist service in St. John 's Anglican Cathedral on Victoria Island, and then on Christmas Day, joined thousands of street people, drug addicts, and recovering drug addicts in Hang Fook Camp on the Hong Kong mainland at St. Stephens Society where Jackie Pullinger had begun a work with these people. What a contrast it was between the high church of St. John's Cathedral and the slums of Hang Fook.

Dr. Samuel, Phyllis, Margie, and Elizabeth then flew to Japan to visit Kobe where Elizabeth had taught prior to moving to Hong Kong. They went on to Kyoto, Hiroshima, and Miya Jima where they stayed in a traditional Japanese inn. At the inn they sat on pillows on the *tatami* (grass mat) floor eating rice, fish, and vegetables with chopsticks off the low table.

It was a well-earned rest from the many years Dr. Samuel had served His Majesty King Sobhuza II, King Mswati III, and the people of Swaziland in many different ways. But *Doketela* Samuel was not finished yet—not by a long shot. Soon he would be taking up his service to His Majesty King Jesus, King of kings and Lord of lords, once again.

15

A CHANGING SOCIETY

Dr. Samuel reflected on ninety years in Swaziland. "It has been an amazing walk to be a part of a country that, when I first arrived, had no electricity. Now it has become an independent nation with an emerging economy and national life. In my childhood days we used kerosene lanterns and candles for light. Then, Mr. Jack Riley, who had a tin mine in the hills near Mbabane, established the very first hydroelectric plant on a small river coming through the capital city of Mbabane and cascading down the Malagwane Mountain. This plant provided power to the tin mine. Slowly the plant's capacity expanded and today South Africa and Swaziland have partnered to build the huge Maguga Dam that supplies water to the farmlands of Hhohho Region and beyond and provides hydroelectricity for the country.

"As a child I do not recall what enterprise or industry may have existed in the country. I do remember Sydney Williams, who came as Director of Education from the UK, to the local Government school in Bremersdorp. He and his family were farmers and had extensive beef, maize, and potato farms. Today their grandchildren run extensive beef and poultry operations.

"Another industry was the Usutu Pulp mill—the brain child of Mr. Shepstone, who was the British High Commissioner in the early days. He saw the potential for the largest manmade forest in the world to be planted to cover the rocky mountains of Swaziland. In the 1960s the first paper pulp mill was imported from the UK. When wood was turned to pulp, it was exported by road to the ocean and then by sea to Japan.

"Rich iron ore of the Ngwenya Mountains to the north of the country was mined and loaded into trains to be transported to Maputo in Mozambique for export to Japan for its steel industry. Japan made a high quality steel from this special type of iron ore.

"Asbestos was mined in Havelock until it was learned that breathing asbestos fibers constituted a serious health hazard. In Dvokolwako there were diamond mines. Coke coal of exceptional quality was mined at Mpaka and exported for steel production in the UK.

"Oranges, grapefruits, and pineapples formed a thriving canning industry for Libby products. All of these developments are part of the transformation we watched with our own eyes as the rural countryside, dotted with clusters of grey-thatched huts forming homesteads changed into the modern five- and ten-story buildings of our cities today.

"There were no telephones in Swaziland when I was a boy. When the first old telephone system was installed, you would wind the little handle on the side of the device a certain number of times so that the person you wanted would be alerted and recognize their ring and so would pick it up. International calls had to be booked weeks in advance. Now I take my cell phone and dial anywhere in the world. In minutes I can speak to the person I'm calling as if they were standing right beside me.

"Written communications traveled by the British Royal Postal Service, and that traveled by stagecoach. Letters took weeks and months to make it from Swaziland to England or Scotland, going first by stagecoach to Breyten, then by rail to Johannesburg, and then on to Durban or Cape Town to be sent by steamship to Southampton, England, or beyond into the UK or Europe. Now we can send emails across the globe to any part of the world in seconds."

By the 1960s Swaziland was beginning to develop and hold its own, educationally, economically, agriculturally, and industrially. The British government donated Parliament Buildings with the Upper and Lower Houses for governance of the Nation. They also gave the National Stadium for Independence Celebrations and the national sport of soccer. His Majesty King Sobhuza II had rallied the Nation to raise funds and build a National Church beside the new Houses of Parliament in Lobamba. Later a National Museum was established, and the National Archives were set in the same vicinity of Lobamba, adjacent to the Royal Residence and seat of the monarchy in Ludzidzini.

The British Protectorate lasted through the reigns of King George IV, V, and VI. As a Protectorate, the British kings were the official Heads of State of Swaziland—the official kings of Swaziland. Dr. David was invited by the British High Commissioner to join a group of men to begin the land handover process for an independent Swaziland. He was on a special commission to the British government to resolve the process of independence. At the time, Mr. Brian Marwick was the British High Commissioner in Swaziland.

In 1968, independence came to Swaziland, and the King was reinstated as His Majesty King Sobhuza II. England, under the reign of Her Majesty Queen Elizabeth II, handed over the Swazi leadership and governance to Him. It was a totally peaceful and orderly transfer, though not everyone was pleased with the two-party political system inherited from the British governance. Independence celebrations involved the schools, police, military, and health services, all displayed themselves as part of the national day of celebration in the new Somhlolo National Stadium.

His Majesty King Sobhuza II gave true respect to the Lord God Almighty's intervention in the Nation and his own Methodist background, having been schooled at a Methodist school in Transkei. The King lifted his Bible on that day and declared this was the Nation's constitution, and on this book the Nation would stand, and in this book the Nation would live. He declared his personal commitment to walk in the footsteps of

Jesus Christ of Nazareth and called the entire Nation to honor His decision by making the same commitment individually.

"King Sobhuza II was a great statesman of kindness, shrewdness, and wisdom, and He was dearly loved by all. It was my privilege to be His attending physician for most of His life and especially in His last ten years as He battled leukemia," Dr. Samuel said. "It was a privilege to set up a small cottage as a special, intensive care unit in the hills of Lobamba Lomdzala where the King was treated for some years. It was a national tragedy when He passed away, and the resultant political insecurity had many ramifications in our lives.

"It was with great delight in 1986 that HRH Prince Makhosetive was inducted and made King of the Nation, the *Ingwenyama*. His name was changed to King Mswati III. Sixteen years earlier, I had no idea that when I was called to the maternity ward because La Twala, the *InKhosikati*, was in labor, that I would actually be bringing into life the future King of the Nation. The present King of this Nation of Swaziland was

King Mswati III lifts up the first release of the Siswati Bible "*LiBhayibheli LeliNgcwele*" and declares that He will follow in His Father's footsteps. He too will search for the footsteps of Jesus Christ of Nazareth. He too will exhort the Nation to "eat the Word of God so that the Nation may live."

born and entered life on earth by my very hands.

"I remember seeing Him when I went on official business to the Embo Palace at Lobamba where the Queen Mother lived. He had a little bicycle and was riding around the palace grounds. I realized then that this was a special little boy. I made a mental note that something was going on here. I kept an eye on this little

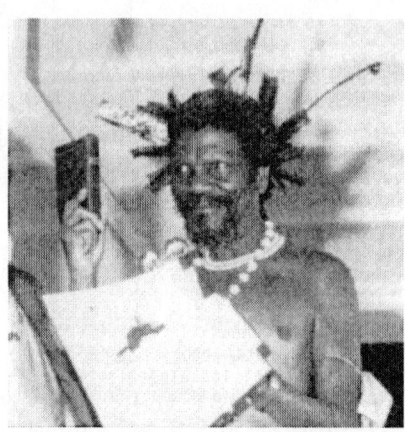

On Independence Day, 6 September 1968, at the Somhlolo National Stadium, King Sobhuza II lifts up the "Umculu," the Holy Bible upon which the Nation will build itself.

boy. He has been my pride and joy in these years of maturation and growth, personally and with His Nation."

As earlier stated, Prince Makhosetive went to school in the United Kingdom for many years in preparation for this leadership position. Even so, He was very young when He was called to take up his father's position in the land. When He took the oath of office, He proudly held up the Holy Bible as His father had done and pledged that He too would walk as His father King Sobhuza II had taught Swazis to walk—in the footsteps of Jesus Christ our Lord and King.

*   *   *

The British system of governance that the Nation had inherited did not serve it well. Swaziland is a small nation of one very big family. To have two opposing political parties was culturally non-workable. When it comes to conflicts with "do this and don't do this," "have this, don't take that," King Sobhuza II was the man with the answers. Just after independence, the King (knowing the constitution inherited from Britain was too western compared to the African way of doing things and was not suitable for the Swazi people and their way of ruling) set

aside the constitution in a very clever way. King Sobhuza II rescinded Parliament in 1972 and suspended the democratic
procedure. He set up commissions to meet with people from
all walks of life to confer as to the needs of the people. That
led to the creation of a unique democratic procedure of representative government.

Dr. Samuel was appointed to the commission that con-
sulted with the people throughout the country. The commission spent a number of years visiting every community and
every chieftainship throughout the country, holding community and town meetings, seeking to bring together the heart
and mind of the Nation as to the type of representative government that would meet the modern world standards of one-
man, one-vote representation, but still maintain the national
identity of Swazi leadership and decision-making.

The King had good relationships with neighboring countries. He was committed to working peacefully and coopera-
tively with Colonial Nations and First Nations. In Mozambique,
He befriended Samora Machel and the Portuguese leaders.
Samora Machel was a Mozambican military commander, rev-
olutionary socialist leader, and eventually the president of
Mozambique. Machel led the country from independence in
1975 until his death in 1986 when his presidential aircraft
crashed in mountainous terrain at the point where the borders
of Mozambique, Swaziland, and South Africa converge.

Later on, His Majesty King Mswati III, called Dr. Samuel
into service to help develop a new political system of elections
and representation. Again the Commission was set up to meet
with every community and every chieftainship for their heartfelt desires and wisdom. After many thousands of hours of
deliberation, debate, and discussion, a very unique political
system evolved. Elections were to be one vote for every citizen
from the age of eighteen and above. Registration was required
prior to the election process.

The first day of elections was for all citizens eighteen years
and older to gather in their constituency (*InKhundla*) to nomi-

nate a representative to parliament. Every person had an equal opportunity to be nominated. If fifteen people signed for a candidate on the nomination ballot, the person was nominated to the election ballot. The second day of elections was to review each candidate who had been nominated and then to vote once for the candidate of choice. The third election day was the final day, and the top three nominees from the previous ballot were voted on again. The winner would then be presented to the local chief of the area, and if the chief found the person was someone he or she could work with, then with the chief's endorsement, the candidate would be sent to represent the people of that constituency in Parliament.

The King also appointed ten people of His personal choice to Parliament. From among the parliamentarians, the King would select half of the Senate, while the second half were appointees to the Senate or an Upper House by election in the Lower House. This somewhat resembled the British Upper and Lower House system. These individuals served as the legislative body of government. Swaziland is to be commended that the Nation has had no revolution or civil war in its history and continues to this day with this simple method of local and national representation in government.

A similar commission was set up under HRH Prince David, a highly respected older brother to King Mswati III, to head up the National Constitution Committee, financed primarily by the British Government to write a formalized National Constitution. After many years of debate and due process Swaziland officially became a Constitutional Monarchy, with the signing of the document by His Majesty upholding the heartfelt commitments and desires of His people.

*   *   *

Being a participant and witness to these changes in Swaziland's history has truly been an amazing and incredible honor for Dr. Samuel. As a British subject, it was an even greater honor for him, his wife, and his three daughters, Elizabeth,

Audrey, and Margaret to be invited in 1968 by His Majesty King Sobhuza II to have full citizenship in Swaziland, when Swaziland resumed its life as an independent Nation.

"Today there are many challenges in the Nation of Swaziland. Yet to think I was crawling on the dirt floor of a kitchen where young men came to learn to read and write and now there are more than 1,500 primary schools and 700 high schools or secondary schools along with numerous tertiary institutions of learning, including the University of Swaziland located in Kwaluseni next to Matsapha Industrial Centre. There is also Southern African Nazarene University bringing the original College of Nursing, College of Education, and Theological Bible College of the Church of the Nazarene into one tertiary institution offering degrees. Recently launched is the Christian Medical and Technology University started by Korean Christian Mission in Mbabane and the Limkokwing Information and Technology University, a branch of the University in Malaysia.

Dr. Samuel received Doctor of Science (honoris causa) in Medicine from the Chancellor of the University of Swaziland, King Mswati III (15 September 2001)

"When I arrived in the country, we travelled by oxcart. I rode a donkey bareback to school. Now we have dual carriageways, asphalt highways, and two international airports, one at Matsapha and the other at Sekuphe. Travel that used to take three days from Johannesburg to Swaziland now takes less than forty-five minutes by jet plane and four hours by road."

His Majesty King Mswati III has honored Dr. Samuel for his commitment and investment in this Nation. At the annual graduation of the University of Swaziland on 15 September 2001,

His Majesty, as Chancellor of the University, conferred upon Dr. Samuel the degree of Doctor of Science, *Honoris Causa*, and at the fortieth anniversary celebrations of the independence of Swaziland on 18 September 2008, His Majesty invested upon him the Order of *Eswatini* in the Kingdom of Swaziland, which is similar to knighthood in the British Commonwealth.

Dr. Samuel W. Hynd stands on the steps of Buckingham Palace in London, England, in 1998 with his CBE (Commander of British Empire) honour given to him by Queen Elizabeth II.

God has given his servant double honor on earth as these honors followed the recognition of the United Kingdom with the investiture of Dr. Samuel Hynd by Queen Elizabeth II at St. James Court in London as Commander of the British Empire (CBE) on 31 December 1998. The Word of God says we will see the goodness of the Lord in the land of the living, and truly this is the way of a life of service, sacrifice, dedication, and honor.

16

A BIRTHDAY DECISION

In 2004, Dr. Samuel celebrated a milestone in his life, his eight-ieth birthday, by announcing a milestone decision. He had de-cided to close the Manzini Medical Centre and spend the rest of his days fighting his last war—a war against HIV/AIDS. What energy he had left would be devoted to helping the fam-ilies of Swaziland who had been devastated by the AIDS pan-demic. Like Caleb of the Bible,[1] he determined to overcome all obstacles despite his age. He would now focus his remaining energies on building a clinic where victims of "the wasting dis-ease," as the Swazis called it, could be treated.

Eightieth birthday cake (1 meter x 1 meter) with an eagle mounting up on its wings over a mountain. This represents the national challenge of Swaziland's HIV/AIDS pandemic yet to be overcome.

His birthday cake represented his vision. It had a huge mountain, like those in Swaziland with an eagle flying over the top. Printed in icing were two scripture references: Isaiah 40:31, KJV ("They that wait upon the Lord shall renew their strength; they shall mount up with wings as eagles; they shall run, and not be weary; and they shall walk, and not faint"); and Joshua 14:9-12 NKJV ("The land where your foot has trodden shall be your inheritance. . . . Now, here I am this day, eighty-five years old. As yet I am strong this day as on the day that Moses sent me. . . . Now therefore, give me this mountain."

Caleb was referring to the mountain held by the Jebusites, the very site that would one day become the city of Jerusalem. However, at that time, no one was bold enough to take out the Jebusites, so eighty-five-year-old Caleb volunteered, once again trusting God for the impossible and seeing the delivering hand of the Lord. Even though this birthday was Dr. Samuel's eightieth, he felt he had the strength of a forty year old. He would take his place to work toward the eradication of HIV/AIDS in Swaziland through the holistic care of the victims and their families.

Once again, as it is for all his patients, he believed that AIDS patients must be treated as whole people. As a doctor, he must fight infections, secondary infections, social stigma, and discrimination. The whole family of the AIDS patient needs to be involved in the treatment. He asked, "How do a husband and wife adjust to this? How do you live with a death warrant? What if you have to change jobs—or what if you lose a job because you are too ill to work? What does a family do?"

For his birthday, a huge tent was set up on the field adjacent to the Sharpe Memorial Church built by his mother. The Prime Minister and Cabinet, old colleagues, and friends were there. His Majesty sent HRH Prince MaHlaba (one of Dr Samuel's best friends) to represent him. Also attending were the Regional Administrator for the Manzini region, a close and dear friend of Dr. Samuel's, HRH Prince Masitsela; the Honorable Dr. Ben Sibandze, former Prime Minister and presently Hhohho Regional Administrator, and also a dear friend to Dr. Samuel—the headman of the Elwandle Community where Dr. Samuel lives. These individuals spoke of the many years of friendship and leadership with their friend and colleague, Dr. Samuel. The president of the Combined League Conference and Council of Churches (SACUC), Reverend Dr. Nicholas Nyawo, was there as were the leaders and pastors of the three church fellowships, the League of Swaziland Churches, the Swaziland Conference of Churches, and the Council of Swaziland Churches. Pastors from the United Kingdom, Reverend Kaye Dimeo and Reverend Paul James, flew out for the occasion. Choirs and groups sang, speakers spoke, and others read poems. These were the organizations, ministries, and services that had been influenced by his life.

The Children of New Hope Centre and students of the Nazarene College of Nursing shared skits and dramas of the work, consultations, and surgeries of the veteran missionary doctor. These skits were hilarious as they enacted some of the funniest events that have been kept in the hearts and memories of patients and colleagues. The Church of the Nazarene leadership and National Board, choirs from churches, the leaders of the Community Health Services, college principals, and leaders of the charities and organizations founded and established by Dr. Samuel, all participated in giving tribute for a life well lived and service well rendered.

Dr. Samuel then began to declare the change in direction that God had placed on his heart. He talked about what the needs of an AIDS patient are. He realized that the treatment of these patients simply was not workable as part of his daily clinic practice. So many people were trying to get in to see him that they were sleeping outside his clinic so they could be first in queue in the mornings. Dr. Samuel had discovered that each patient needed two hours or more for an appointment. If he gave each one that much time, there was no time left for his regular patients. He decided the only solution was an HIV clinic where he could focus on the specific needs of these patients and not take time from his other patients who did not have the disease.

*   *   *

Audrey and Elizabeth, his daughters sat down with him to brainstorm the idea of a clinic devoted solely to the treatment of AIDS, they decided that first and foremost, the clinic must be welcoming. There had to be a reception area where the person was welcomed, registered, and taken in for counseling. There must be easy access. In addition, there needed to be a place for pre-test counseling, blood testing, and post-test counseling. Each patient would see a doctor who would set up a protocol for treatment. They realized that most patients come for some condition other than AIDS. In fact, it is a rather common belief among Swazis that no one has AIDS—at least not in the beginning.

Dr. Samuel and Dr. Elizabeth, along with some others in Swaziland, were invited to become part of a consortium of health care practices in the Southeastern Africa corridor, involving Mpumalanga (the Eastern Province of South Africa), Kwa-Zulu Natal, Swaziland, and the southern portion of Mozambique. The first meeting of this consortium was held at the ACTS Community Clinic (ACTS meaning AIDS Care Training and Support) near the town of White River in Mpumalanga. There, Dr. Samuel found that the clinic Dr. Margie Hardman had recently opened was based on the exact same principles and procedures he had brainstormed with this daughters. Dr. Margie showed him around her red brick clinic that had two consulting rooms, a reception area, a pharmacy, and a training centre.

Later on, Dr. Margie came to Manzini to see the land where a new AIDS clinic would be built. When it was completed, Dr. Samuel named the clinic ACTS II because Dr. Margie's clinic was ACTS I. Dr. Margie is an amazing woman who has become a major speaker on the subject of how to care for AIDS patients with treatment and support. Both clinics upheld John

10:10 as their purpose. "I have come that you might have life and have it more abundantly."

Dr. Margie Hardman and Rev. Harry Munnings, founders of ACTS Clinic in White River, South Africa, make a site visit at ACTS II. They came to pray for the vision and establishment of ACTS II Community Clinic. (Also in the photo are Elizabeth Hynd and Caroline Ferguson.)

It was 1989 when Dr. Samuel saw his first case of AIDS. "One of the top people from the sugar estate, a secretary, was in my office. I examined her, and I could see all her symptoms fit those of AIDS. She definitely had the disease," Dr. Samuel said. "She was my first case. It is reported that sixty-five percent of the sugar estate workforce are HIV positive. The workers are separated from their families by great distances. These lonely people seek companionship to ease loneliness, and the search to ease their loneliness often includes sexual relationships. When I told this patient that she was positive, she was stunned. That was *my* first case of AIDS, but the first *documented* case of AIDS in Swaziland was diagnosed in 1986-87, three years before I saw this woman."

For a long time no one in Swaziland would admit the Nation had a problem. Even the Prime Minister speaking in the Somhlolo Stadium in 1989 publically denied the Nation had a problem. It was not until the confirmed cases were above twenty-seven percent that officials acknowledged something serious was happening. At that point His Majesty began seeking help from the United States and Europe to help with diagnosis, care, and treatment of those afflicted by the virus.

*   *   *

When he knew what he wanted to build, Dr. Samuel went to leaders of the Church of the Nazarene to see if he could use a small piece of their land for a clinic. There was a small acreage within walking distance of a huge population of transient people. Thirty-five thousand people lived in the temporary settlement area of Mahlabatsini. These are farmers and herdsmen who came to the area seeking jobs in industry. Finding no jobs, they put up temporary shelters. As time passed, they still did not find jobs, yet they stayed, and the settlement became a hotbed of disease. AIDS is prevalent there.

When the church heard the story, they gave Dr. Samuel permission to build on the land. Next he had to go to His Majesty King Mswati III for His permission to build the clinic, because even though the land belonged by title deed to the Nazarenes, still all land belongs to the King. His Majesty King Mswati III understood the magnitude of the problem his Nation was and is facing. The King readily gave permission to build the facility. Currently, Dr. Samuel has asked for more land, and the King has sent him to a man who can make a land transfer happen. The transaction has not been completed at the time of this writing.

In the beginning of the pandemic, there was no AIDS registry. There were only registries for malaria and TB. Now, however, AIDS patients are tracked. Swaziland has a lot of TB as it goes along with AIDS because AIDS compromises the immune system. Swaziland still has the highest HIV/AIDS infection rate (percentage of the population—25.8% of all adults) in the world. The average life expectancy has dropped from sixty-seven years of age to forty-seven years. So a large part of the clinic's work is to educate people about AIDS—how the disease is spread and the precautions people must take to prevent infecting other family members.

Dr. Samuel began to raise funds for the new clinic that would not only treat the whole person through education, drug treatment, support, and home-based care but also treat the aftermath of the disease—orphans and widows.

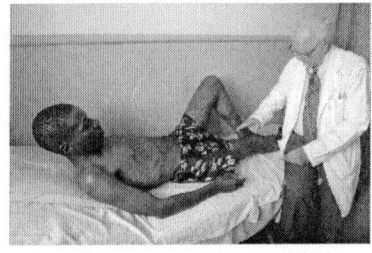

Caring for the whole person, male and female.

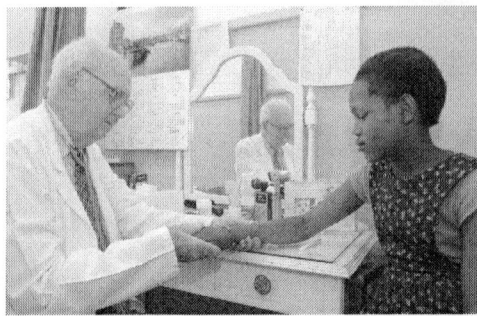

Children tell their stories as he cares for young and old.

Dr. Elizabeth Hynd was invited to Ottawa, Canada, to speak on the "aftermath of HIV/AIDS" (the plight and proposed solutions to assist orphaned and vulnerable children) at an International HIV/AIDS Conference held there. This conference dealt with the three major challenges of the pandemic: the educational aspect toward the reduction of the rate of infection (prevention); the care and treatment of those infected with HIV/AIDS; and the aftermath of widows and the orphaned and vulnerable children. Her speech followed the same vision as her father of treating the whole person.

She returned and Dr. Samuel and friends in Nelspruit helped draft a proposal applying for Canadian International Development Agency (CIDA) funds for building the ACTS II Clinic. Brian and Anne Souter, in Scotland, gave funds for operational and environmental permissions and procedures. The congregation at Southbrook Christian Community Church in Dayton, Ohio, collected a special offering of their jewelry, class rings, and the like, and then melted down their gold and silver, sold it, and gave the proceeds for the construction of the clinic. Silver Angels, a group of retired medical practitioners from Canada, raised funds and then came to Swaziland on a mission trip. Together with the teenagers of New Hope Centre, they painted the walls and restored used furniture for the Clinic. Melanie and Glen Stansfield, Canadian friends, gave of their resources. The US Embassy Self Help Grant provided other needed furniture and equipment. The Embassy of Japan gave a custom-built Toyota Quantum to transport patients and supplies. The American Embassy in Swaziland gave all the in-

ACTS II Community Clinic; the vision becomes a reality and operates to serve the community on 3 January 2011.

digenous plants from their new embassy building site. The finished clinic now treats fifty to eighty patients per day.

* * *

ACTS II Community Clinic team of doctors, nurses, counselors, administrative and support staff.

Dr. Samuel has dedicated his life to taking care of the body so that the spirit and soul have a place to live. "That's why I've done what I've done for nearly all of my ninety years," he says. "I've seen malaria, leprosy, smallpox, and other infectious diseases dealt with—for all intents and purposes, they are no more. Now I want to live to see AIDS eradicated.

"While many anti-retroviral drugs have been developed, and while there is a better understanding of how to treat the disease through nutrition and drugs, a full-blown cure has eluded scientists so far."

Thinking back over the many years of his practice, he said, "I have seen those who were saved and healed at the RFM Hospital. Many times those patients asked for a church to be built in their home community before they asked for a clinic. Even now, at this time of writing, I am still building clinics in three places in the south of Swaziland.

"I served as Grantee of schools and on the steering committee of the Southern African University, seeing the soul of a person nurtured from preschool to tertiary education. I have built and established so many church congregations and church buildings that I could not begin to name or even count them.

"I recall that when the Motjane area was being developed as a community and industrial site near the northern border of our country, I approached the committees responsible in government to request church sites in the area before any roads or buildings had been built. God graciously touched the hearts of two congregations in the United States who contacted me to say they wanted to build a church in Swaziland. We were approved for the two sites. We built the churches even before any houses were built in those areas. Today those two flourishing churches still exist and you can see them from the main highway as you enter the country through the Oshoek northern border gate.

"I was approached by another church in the USA that wanted to build a clinic in the same area as the first church, so I approached the committee and they designated a site for the clinic. As I was Minister of Health at the time, I was able to arrange for the International Director of WHO (World Health Organization) from Geneva to come and open the facility. Poor man, we were deluged with freezing cold rain that day, but the clinic was officially opened and still operates, serving that community today.

"So while I thank God that I have been able to do all these things, I still want to see AIDS conquered and the tide of death from this disease in Swaziland turned away. I want to see a Nation whole and healthy. I want children to have their parents to raise them. I want teachers, police officers, judges, lawyers, doctors, nurses, and a whole host of professionals who have died of AIDS to be replaced by a new generation that is free of this disease. I want this pandemic to stop, and by God's grace, it will. And you, dear reader, can make it a matter of constant prayer, and together we will see victory come."

God is on our side, "an ever present help in times of trouble."
(A little humour helps a long way.)

Note

1. Joshua 14:6-12 NIV: Now the people of Judah approached Joshua at Gilgal, and Caleb son of Jephunneh the Kenizzite said to him, "You know what the LORD said to Moses the man of God at Kadesh Barnea about you and me. I was forty years old when Moses the servant of the LORD sent me from Kadesh Barnea to explore the land. And I brought him back a report according to my convictions, but my fellow Israelites who went up with me made the hearts of the people melt in fear. I, however, followed the LORD my God wholeheartedly. So on that day Moses swore to me, "The land on which your feet have walked will be your inheritance and that of your children forever, because you have followed the LORD my God wholeheartedly."

AN ONGOING STORY

"The world is losing itself," Dr. Samuel muses. "Where do you see people thinking about things and saying, 'This is the right thing to do'? When my wife, Rosemarie, heard about living in a mud hut, she did not quiver or waiver. She came willingly to Swaziland because it was the right thing to do.

"My concern is; how do we meet the present-day situation? Everyone is saying, 'Where are we going?' and none of them know. What I see on television is disturbing because it is just froth. With all our modern gadgetry, I have to ask, where are we going?

"Where is Swaziland going in the future? I believe Swaziland has a bright future. We are ahead of other nations because the rest of the world hasn't caught on to what really matters. For example: There is still a closeness to the vision of King Somhlolo—a leaning toward the things of God in our country. There is still satisfaction in improving this Nation. His Majesty dreams of achieving first world Nation status by 2022, and we eagerly watch as developments, such as the Science and Technology Park currently being built, are developed. This is one of the unfolding steps toward the dream becoming a reality."

Swaziland has a destiny in God's plan for the nations. When God spoke the words in Somhlolo's vision that the Nation should "eat the book on the inside and the Nation would live," God implied that once we tasted the good news of salvation, we would preach it and live it among the nations. Dr. Samuel believes that Swaziland is the "Pulpit of Africa" and will bring the Good News to the nations. Trans World Radio (TWR) is a multinational evangelical Christian media distributor. It is the largest Christian media organization in the world and it beams the Gospel on the radio airwaves to 160 countries in more than 230 languages and dialects. Swaziland is one of the organization's major transmitting sites. So the Word of God goes out from this station and this Nation and the dream in the heart of God is that Swaziland will be the pulpit of Africa will become a reality.

Dr. Samuel says, "I'm still dreaming about what could be done here for the clinic. I want to add two wings on the ACTS II Clinic for patients too sick to wait on the verandah, as they do now. Sometimes it gets windy and cold out there. I want a place to X-ray patients and also a blood lab. Now people have to go to RFM Hospital for tests and X-rays. It would be so much better if we had everything right at the clinic.

"His Majesty has, at the time of this printing, assigned His secretary to arrange for a site meeting to designate the land that would be needed to complete the developments for this vision to flourish. We are currently waiting for the designated men to come on site. This will give us the space to develop the Home Based Care Unit, the two wings of the Main clinic, the training centre, the lab and Xray as well as housing for the tean who will work with us. It will be exciting to see the full development come to pass. Not only do His Majesty's men have their part to play, many others will be needed to raise funds, to develop infrastructure, and select and train the team to function in compassion and professionalism.

"So where is the project the Lord has given *you* to complete? Are you in the dirt floor phase? The Stone Church phase? The attracting partners phase? Or have you moved on to affect those beyond your local community? No matter where you are, don't despise humble beginnings. God can use you too.

"My father, Dr. David, often asked people to do more than they thought they possibly could. He expressed confidence in us and gave us a task and the means to accomplish it. Once we took that small step, God spoke to us about taking more steps in that new direction. I challenge you to do likewise in your life. Express confidence in people; then give them a task and the means to accomplish it. Don't do it for them. God delights in using those who take the first small step. You might be the one being challenged by a new or unexpected task. Be confident and step out in faith. A life dedicated to service begins with a life given to God.

"When you hear God's call, simply answer: '*Here am I! Send me*'" (Isaiah 6:8 NKJV).

Dr. Samuel in his little black car—ever moving forward in his vision and dream of overcoming HIV/AIDS in Swaziland.

Award of Excellence

KINGDOM OF SWAZILAND

TO ALL AND SINGULAR TO WHOM THESE PRESENTS SHALL COME,

Greetings,

His Majesty King Mswati III

Has invested and by these presents do invest

The Order of Eswatini

Dr. Samuel Hynd

I hereby authorize you to have, hold and enjoy
the said dignity and rank of
Commander of the aforesaid Order together with all
and singular the privileges
hereunto belonging or appertaining.
As witness by my sign manual
This 18th day of September, 2008.

His Majesty King Mswati III

*****

CBE

COMMANDER OF THE BRITISH EMPIRE

ELIZABETH R

Elizabeth the Second, by the grace of God of the United Kingdom of Great Britain and Northern Ireland and of her other realms and territories, Queen, Head of the Commonwealth, Defender of the Faith and Sovereign of the Most Excellent Order of the British Empire to our trusty and beloved Samuel Wilson Hynd, Esquire

Greetings

Whereas we have thought fit to nominate and appoint you to be an Ordinary Commander of the Civil Division of our said Most Excellent Order of the British Empire.

We do by these presents grant unto you the dignity of an Ordinary Commander of the said Order and hereby authorize you to have and hold and enjoy the said dignity and rank of an Ordinary Commander of our aforesaid Order together with all and singular privileges thereunto belonging or appertaining.

Given at our Court at St. James under our Sign manual and the Seal of our said Order this 31st day of December 1998 in the 47th year of our reign.

By the Sovereign's Command
Grand Master
Grant of the Dignity of an Ordinary Commander of the Civil Division of the Order of the British Empire

To Samuel Wilson Hynd

MASA

Medical Association South Africa

CREDO

I, a Medical Doctor of the Medical Association of South Africa,

Believe in the sanctity of life and in the promotion of optimal quality of life for all.

I will therefore strive

To use my **knowledge and skills** to promote and protect the health of my fellow Human Beings,

To place **medical care above consideration** of race, gender creed, social standing, political allegiance or nature of disease,

To foster a **good relationship** with my patients based on mutual respect communication and trust,

To respect the **rights of my patients**, including the right to informed consent,

To respect the **confidentiality of information** entrusted to me,

To **recognize my limitations** and consult with or refer to my colleagues when necessary,

To maintain and improve my **professional skills,**

To respect and protect the **rights of my colleagues,**

To sustain and promote **integrity, insight, and a caring nature** within the medical profession.

Caring for doctors who care

10 June 1950

SwaziMed

Dependable, Affordable Health Care Coverage

30 year Certificate of Recognition

Awarded to Dr Samuel Hynd in honour being the
founder and being a founding member
and his distinguished contributions to the Fund

11 May 2011

Chairman

*   *   *   *   *

Church of the Nazarene Swaziland
Long Service Award Certificate

This certificate is awarded to

Dr. Samuel W Hynd

For long time service in Evangelism, Education & Health as
honour for

"Keeping the Holistic Gospel Burning"

11 August 2010

National Board Chairman

National Board Secretary

*   *   *   *   *

Salvation Army Southern Africa Territory
Certificate of Appreciation

Presented Dr. Samuel Hynd
In recognition of the valuable Service
Given to the Salvation Army
Appreciate your valuable support and contribution

30 May 2007

Territorial Commander

Administrator

* * * * *

25 Year Silver Jubilee
Cheshire Homes of Swaziland

HONOUR

Dr. Samuel Hynd

For Outstanding Contribution to the Inception of the Organization

13 October 2011

Patron , Her Royal Highness InKhosikati LaNtenteza

Chairperson, Maggie De Waal

Whereas the Director and the Editorial Board of the International Biographical Centre of Cambridge England have ordered the honouring of Distinguished Individual

Dr. Samuel Wilson Hynd, C.B.E.

In that the foreshortened entry posted opposite is included unabridged in the prestigious title

"A LIFETIME ACHIEVEMENT 100"

Published with all due ceremony in the year 2014 in order that they may receive recognition both of their achievements and their contributions to Society and to the International Biographic Centre

Therefore let it be known by this Order the individual is confirmed as an inaugural entrant in Lifetime of Achievement 100 signed at the Centre's headquarters in Cambridge England

Director General

11 August 2004

*   *   *   *   *

Dr. SAMUEL WILSON HYND, C.B.E.

Medical doctor Samuel Wilson Hynd was born on 18 December, 1024 in Glasgow, Scotland. He married Rosemarie Ballard and they had three daughters. Following his first wife's death in a motor accident, he married Phyllis June McNiel in 1976, who was Principal of the Nazarene Nursing College attached to Raleigh Fitkin Memorial Hospital.

At the University of Witwatersrand in South Africa, Samuel Hynd earned his BSc in 1943. He returned to Scotland and achieved his MB ChB in 1949 at the University of Glasgow. The following year he successfully completed his Diploma of Tropical Medicine and Hygiene at the Royal College of Physicians in London, England. Dr. Hynd served as an Intern at the Western Infirmary in Glasgow, Scotland, and between 1950 to 1978 served as a medical officer and then Medical Superintendent at the RFM Hospital of the Church of the Nazarene in Manzini, Swaziland. Since 1978, Dr. Hynd has been Medical Director of the Manzini Medical Centre in Swaziland. During this time he has served as the Minister of Health and Parliament 1978 to 1984 and been Physician to the Royal Family of the Kingdom of Swaziland.

Dr. Hynd has written numerous articles of Professions, Educational and Christian Publications and Magazines. He is the co-author of a Medical Text book entitled Clinical Medicine and Health in Developing Africa having written a section on Leprosy. In honour of his achievements, Dr. Hynd has received many awards. In 1999 he was a Commander of the British Empire (C.B.E.) and he holds the position of Chief Counselor of the Royal Order of King Sobhuza II of Swaziland. He is also a Paul Harris Fellow of the Rotary Club and in 2001 was presented with an Honorary Doctorate of Science, honoris causa, by the University of Swaziland.

In the course of his career, Dr. Hynd has been involved in many professional and local organizations, reflecting his concerns and interests. He is a founder and chairman of the National Council on Smoking, Alcohol and Drug Dependence (COSAD) in Swaziland, and a founder and member of the Coordinating Assembly of Non-Governmental Organizations (CANGO) in Swaziland. Dr. Hynd is a former president and member of the Medical and Dental Council of Swaziland and the Medical and Dental Association of Swaziland, a member of the Christian Medical and Dental Fellowships of the UK, South Africa and USA, and a coordinator of the Christian Medical and Dental Fellowship of Swaziland. He is also founder of the Africa Cooperative Action Trust (Rural Development) and of the Boys' and Girls' Brigade of Swaziland. Dr. Hynd is a long time member of the Leprosy Mission Council of Southern Africa and Charter member of the Rotary Club in Swaziland.

*   *   *   *   *

2000 Outstanding Intellectuals
of the 21st Century

This is to certify that Dr. Samuel Wilson Hynd, C.B.E.,

MB., ChB.

Is Included in

2000 Outstanding Intellectuals of the 21st Century

Second Edition

In Honour of an Outstanding Contribution in the field of

Health, Education and Christian Activities

Signed and Sealed at the International Biographical Centre
Cambridge, England

Authorized Officer
29 October, 2002

*   *   *   *   *

University of Swaziland

We hereby declare by virtue of the authority
vested in the Council and Senate through the Statutes
of the University of Swaziland that on those of
exceptional merit or for those who for any reason seem
worthy, we may confer the dignities and privileges of
Doctor in accordance with this Principle, it is now our
pleasure to confer upon

Samuel Wilson Hynd

The Degree of

DOCTOR OF SCIENCE

Honoris causa

Vice Chancellor   Rector

Makhubela   Vilakati

15th day of September, 2001

*   *   *   *   *

The Outstanding Holiness Leadership Award

For 2002

Is presented to

Dr. Samuel W Hynd

In recognition of 25 years of Service to
Swaziland Nazarene Bible College

Through encouragement, promotion and dedicated
financial support

7 December, 2002

*   *   *   *   *

The National Council on Smoking, Alcohol and Drug Dependence, Swaziland

COSAD

Confers on

Dr. Samuel W Hynd

A life Membership in COSAD

As founding Member of COSAD and for his outstanding service as Chairman of COSAD from 1984 to 2001

Executive Director
Chairman

22nd May, 2001

*   *   *   *   *

"But for you who revere my name, the Son of Righteousness will rise with healing in its wings…"Malachi 4:2

Operation Sunrise Africa

Certificate of Appreciation
Awarded to
Dr. Samuel Hynd

In recognition of the surpassing dedication and commitment you have demonstrated in helping fulfill the vision of O.S.A. to reach with the Gospel of Our Lord Jesus Christ 50 million people in 50 major cities of Southern and Eastern Africa in the 50 day period of running from 1st July to 19th August 2002

With Sincere Appreciation

Bekele Shanko, Area Director 31st December, 2002
National Director

*   *   *   *   *

This Certificate of Inclusion Commemorates the
Achievements of

Dr. Samuel W. Hynd

Which are listed in the First Edition of

The Contemporary Who's Who

Selected for Inclusion on the basis of

*Merited accomplishments and success in
Contemporary Society*

1st September, 2002
C.A. Mitchell, Editor in Chief

*   *   *   *   *

Christian Medical and Dental Association

Hereby certify that

Samuel W. Hynd, M.D.

Has become a lifetime member of the Christian Medical and Dental Associations and has fully subscribed to its ideals and principles

President
2001
Secretary

**Christian Medical and Dental Associations,
Changing Hearts in Health Care**

*   *   *   *   *

Church of the Nazarene

Certificate of Recognition

Dr. Samuel Hynd

In recognition of your faithful and special
contributions to the life and liveliness of the
Mbabane Church of the Nazarene

TO GOD BE THE GLORY

Rev Grace Masilela   S. Maphanga
Senior Pastor   Secretary

5th May 2012

*   *   *   *   *

Award of Distinction

Presented to

Dr. Samuel Wilson Hynd

For 26 years of outstanding service and commitment to the Lord Jesus Christ and the poor and needy of Swaziland.

A true Man of God who went far beyond the call of duty.

Chairman of ACAT Swaziland established 1982 until 2008
A.C.A.T. Swaziland

Those who excel ultimately outshine their achievements, thank you for everything you do!

"Let your light so shine before men that they may see your good works and glorify your father who is in heaven" Matt. 5:16

*   *   *   *   *

Award of Excellency

The position of Honorary Chairman is awarded to

Dr. Samuel W. Hynd

In recognition of his valuable contributions
to the establishment, development and
guidance of

ACAT-Lilima Swaziland (1982-2008)

On this 2nd Day of December, 2008

Trustees: Rev Dr. C.P.M. Gumede, Dr. B.M.Nsibandze,
Mrs A.L.Dlamini, Mr M.J.Simelane

*   *   *   *   *

International Biographical Centre

IBC

LIFETIME ACHIEVEMENT AWARD

This certificate commemorates and celebrates the life and work of

Samuel Wilson Hynd

Who has met and exceeded the criteria set by the awards board of the International Biographic Centre and as such has been presented with the IBC Lifetime Achievement Award on the date given below in recognition of an Outstanding Contribution to

Medicine

Duly signed by the Director General, this certificate bears the seal of the IBC and is
due testament to the dedication of the recipient and is recorded in the annals of the
headquarters of the International Biographic Centre, Cambridge, England.

March 2003.

*   *   *   *   *

This warrant proclaims that the undersigned

Dr. Samuel Wilson Hynd, CBE

Has been included in the Dedications Section of

Living Legends

In honour of an outstanding contribution to

Health Services, Education, Community Development

Director General   Editor in Chief

20th November 2003

Date of Proclamation

International Biographical Centre

Cambridge, England

*   *   *   *   *

The First Royal World Tour

Of

His Majesty King Mswati III with

InKhosikati LaNgangazi

October 6th to 28th, 1989

To all participants an award of Thanks

To Dr. Samuel W Hynd of

Elwandle, Manzini, Swaziland.

His Majesty King Mswati III Historic Speech

at the 44th General Assembly of the

United Nations

12th October, 1989

*   *   *   *   *

Diamond Jubilee

1921-1981

King Sobhuza II
Sovereign Head of State of the
Kingdom of Swaziland

Honours and awards the faithful service of His Cabinet

The Honourable Dr. Samuel Wilson Hynd

Minister of Health

6th September, 1981

*   *   *   *   *

The American Biographical Institute

Presents

Samuel Wilson Hynd

With its 2003 COMMEMORATIVE MEDAL
In recognition of his selection as

Man of the Year

For outstanding community and professional achievement.

Registered in the Institutes Library and Archives in the
United States of America
Sanctioned by the Board of International Research with
their signatures herewith.

Limited Issue #32
J.M.Evans & L.M.Kellander

*   *   *   *   *

One of the major and leading authorities on the
biographies of distinguished individuals world wide,
the American Biographical Institute , U.S.A.
does hereby proclaim that . . .

Dr. Samuel Wilson Hynd

Has been selected as

MAN OF THE YEAR
2002

*Based on his outstanding accomplishments to
date and the noble example he has set for his peers
and entire community*

Sanctioned by the American Biographical Institute and
its Board of International Research
Registrar L. M. Kellander
Member Governing Board of Editors, C. L. White

*   *   *   *   *

Scroll of Legend

This scroll proudly proclaims the presence of

Dr. Samuel Wilson Hynd, CBE

Within the inaugural edition of Living Legends
published in the year two thousand and three by the
International Biographical Centre
In honour of their outstanding contributions in

Health and Social Services
in Swaziland

Signed and Sealed at the headquarters of the IBC,
Cambridge England.

20th May, 2003
Director General Authorized Officer

*   *   *   *   *

Awards Made to Dr. David Hynd

OBE
ORDER OF THE BRITISH EMPIRE

GEORGE R VI

George the Sixth, by the grace of God of Great Britain, Ireland and the British Dominions beyond the Seas. King, Defender of the Faith, Emperor of India and Sovereign of the Most Excellent Order of the British Empire to our trusty and beloved David Hynd, Esquire

Greetings

Whereas we have thought fit to nominate and appoint you to be an Additional Officer of the Civil Division of our said Most Excellent Order of the British Empire.

We do by these presents grant unto you the dignity of an Ordinary Commander of the said Order of the British Empire. We do by these presents grant unto you the dignity of an Additional Officer of our said Order together with all and singular privileges thereunto belonging or appertaining.

Given at our Court at St James under our Sign manual and the Seal of our said Order this 11th day of May 1937 in the 1st year of our reign.

By the Sovereign's Command
Grand Master

Grant of the Dignity of an Additional Officer
of the Civil Division of the Order of the British Empire

To David Hynd, Esquire, M.B.,Ch.B.

CBE
COMMANDER OF THE BRITISH EMPIRE

GEORGE R VI

George the Sixth, by the grace of God of Great Britain, Ireland and the British Dominions beyond the Seas. King, Defender of the Faith, Emperor of India and Sovereign of the Most Excellent Order of the British Empire to our trusty and beloved David Hynd, Esquire, Officer of our said most excellent Order

Greetings

Whereas we have thought fit to nominate and appoint you to be an Additional Commander of the Civil Division of our said Most Excellent Order of the British Empire.

We do by these presents grant unto you the dignity of an Additional Commander of the said Order of the British Empire. We do by these presents grant unto you the dignity of an Additional Commander of our said Order together with all and singular privileges thereunto belonging or appertaining.

Given at our Court at St James under our Sign manual and the Seal of our said Order this 1st day of January, 1946 in the 10th year of our reign.

By the Sovereign's Command
Grand Master

Grant of the Dignity of an Additional Commander
of the Civil Division of the Order of the British Empire

To David Hynd, Esquire, M.B.,Ch.B.

The University of Swaziland

Dr. David Hynd

Was awarded the Honorary Degree of

DOCTOR OF LAWS

(Honoris Causa)

On the 12th Day of September 1987.

Vice Chancellor

Makhubela

Registrar

Simelane

KINGDOM OF SWAZILAND

Sobhuza the Second

Of the Kingdom of Swaziland

Sovereign of the Royal Order of Sobhuza II
to my trusty and well beloved

David Hynd

Greetings

Whereas I have thought fit to nominate and appoint
you to be Counsellor
Of the said Royal Order of Sobhuza II
I do by these presents to authorize you to hold and enjoy the said Dignity and Rank thereunto belonging to
appertaining to the said Order

Given at the Royal Court at Lozithehlezi this 22nd Day
of July 1982 in the 61st year of my Reign
By the Sovereign Command

Grant of the dignity of
Counsellor of the Royal Order of Sobhuza II
To David Hynd

To Donate to ACTS II Clinic

By Electronic Transfer:

Bank: Nedbank, Swaziland

Account Name: ACTS II COMMUNITY CLINIC

Branch Name: Manzini

Branch Number: 360264

Account Number: 040000280803

SWIFT Code: NESWSZMX

Donate online via Global Giving platform (credit card or Paypal)

http://www.globalgiving.org/projects/community-outreach-for-hiv-testing-an-treatment/

Tax receipts can be sent to USA givers.
Enter the amount of your gift, and you will also have the option of sending a one-time gift or a monthly recurring gift.